Evans Modern Teaching

Structure in Early Learning

Evans Modern Teaching

Structure in Early Learning

Alice Yardley

Principal Lecturer in Education,
Nottingham College of Education

Evans Brothers Limited   London

Published by Evans Brothers Limited
Montague House
Russell Square, London WC1

60135

Filmset in 11 on 12 point Imprint by
Photoprint Plates Limited, Rayleigh, Essex
and printed in Great Britain by
T. & A. Constable Limited, Edinburgh

ISBN 0 237 29108 8

PRA 3890

Contents

Introduction

In recent years the evolutionary growth of ideas about the education of young children has found expression primarily in the organisation of the environment, of the children themselves and of the day, and in the way in which learning is approached. Comparatively little attention has been paid to the content of the child's curriculum and to the way in which learning situations are structured. Teachers know what to provide and how to promote active learning, and are highly skilled in establishing a helpful intellectual and emotional atmosphere, yet many still depend on assignment cards, work cards, work books and similar extension of formal tuition as a means of ensuring the systematic development of ideas, or progressive learning through the materials provided.

Many teachers realise that the most effective way to maximise the learning opportunity in a situation is to structure it in a way which leads the child from his grasp of simple, familiar ideas towards an ever deepening knowledge and comprehension of what a situation can offer. They also realise that it is far more effective to structure a learning situation from within than to apply external structure by means of instruction cards.

In the days when learning centred on a limited number of prescribed goals, a step-by-step syllabus provided the teacher with a sequence of stages through which she guided the child. Today we hold more liberal views of education and our objectives are always related to the individual child rather than to circumscribed achievements. The term 'unstructured' has been used to describe a way of working which is unfettered by a fixed syllabus, and this has led in some instances to gross misinterpretation of the learning situation. That the child is left free to design his own work pattern certainly does not mean that his learning has no structure. Indeed, the greater the freedom extended to the individual, the greater the need for thoughtful structure in every aspect of his environment, and the key to such structure is our knowledge of the way in which the child's learning develops.

Teachers today know a great deal about the child and the way in which he develops and learns, but most of them would admit that they have a long way to go before they are fully confident of their ability to relate developmental knowledge to everything they do in the classroom. It is in structuring the learning situation and in assessing and recording the child's progress that developmental knowledge may be most effectively applied.

This book examines ways in which our knowledge of the child's conceptual development may be used to provide a framework of ideas and of concrete situations related to these ideas, with reference to different aspects of the environment. We shall also consider realistic modes of assessing and recording the child's progress.

By referring more specifically to the experiences of children during their first years in school, we shall try to define some basic principles which apply to various aspects of the child's early learning. Examples of what happens between children, whose ages range from four plus to eight, and their teachers will be used to illustrate the points made.

While focusing on the child's educational opportunities in school, we should remember that what takes place there must be understood within the context of all that the child learns both inside and outside school, and that in order to complete the structure we must help parents to co-operate in establishing continuity and progression in every aspect of the child's growth and development.

Chapter 1

The need for structure

Teachers in Britain make an exceptionally good job of providing materials and situations which are closely related to the needs and interests of children. While provision is good, close examination of what children are doing, particularly in some parts of the classroom, raises grave doubts about the quality and continuity of their learning. Teachers themselves are worried. 'How is it,' they ask, 'when the provision is good, that learning, sometimes after an auspicious start, comes to a halt, or remains superficial?' Discriminating observers find much to criticise, and sometimes modern principles are brought into disrepute when in fact the problem lies in the inadequacies of the situation rather than in the procedure itself. We have gone a long way in relating principles to practice, but not by any means far enough, and the key to the problem lies in well-organised learning.

The need for systematic planning applies to every aspect of the environment if it is to offer the child educative experience as opposed to mere activity, and there is a vast difference between learning through vital play activities and merely playing about with this and that.

The house corner, for example, can open the way to many types

1

of profitable learning, or it can degenerate into a fort manned by belligerent boys. Water and sand can offer an intellectual challenge, or provide ammunition for a flinging contest. Paint and clay can be vehicles of inspired ideas, or become materials which pass the time with dull results. The dressing-up corner may be a source of highly communicative dramatic play, or a place where a young child wearing a policeman's helmet becomes a serious threat to law and order. Even the investigation table, which should persistently stimulate and satisfy the child's burning curiosity, may be abandoned in favour of some passive activity such as following the instructions accompanying a 'constructional' toy.

When children react in this way, it is small wonder that teachers begin to lose confidence in the child's ability to learn through the pursuit of his natural interests. They may resort to work cards, daily assignments associated with systematic reading and mathematics schemes, or even fall back on formal instruction as the only way to ensure that children learn what they should. Teachers are responsible people, and deeply aware of the significance of their work in shaping future citizens. They are rarely allowed adequate time and help in evaluating newer ways of working, and inevitably they are tempted to fall back on what they know produces socially acceptable results, even though those results may be seriously circumscribed.

This anxiety is most noticeable in the teaching of literacy and numeracy skills, and there are many schools in which reading is singled out for formal treatment, even though other aspects of learning proceed along liberal lines. A carefully regulated reading scheme, accompanied by a systematic check-list of small-step achievements, helps teachers to feel safe, and although they acknowledge the literary inadequacy of the material, they cling to the lifeline it offers. Such a lifeline may serve a useful purpose for the less experienced teacher, but the teacher who is confident in her skill knows that there is a better way if only she had time to work it out.

Similarly, when dealing with mathematical ideas teachers know that there is an aspect of mathematics in every situation, and that children learn through understanding when they meet the need for mathematics in everyday activities. Some teachers explore the possibilities of 'the new maths' and retain what they refer to as 'the old maths' as a safeguard against missing out in the acquisition of essential numeracy skills. Others depend on commercially produced work books and apparatus. In pursuit of the reassuring results which guide books and work cards bring, many opportunities presented by the individual child get pushed aside, and while what he learns may be sound enough, what he could learn we may never know. Knowledgeable use of well-structured mathematical apparatus plays an important part in helping children to formulate ideas, but such material is not a substitute for the real-life problem in which mathematical thinking is demanded of the child.

Those teachers who do recognise the need for well-structured learning situations tend to think in terms of academic work. They may go so far as to plan with great care the child's progress through reading, writing and number activities, yet pay little attention to the child's non-verbal modes of communication, or to what he does with his natural materials. The child's explorations and discoveries may also be left to chance, and a great deal of learning is lost to the child. By concentrating on words and numbers the child may lose out on his academic skills too, for to use literary and numerical symbols exclusively before the child is at ease with them may damage his chances of ever using them with confidence.

If the modern classroom is to offer each child the opportunity to learn at his best rate and to learn what will enable him to maximise his potential, structure based on developmental knowledge must relate to every aspect of learning. This does not mean that teachers resort to putting the child through a programme based on formal instruction, but rather that teachers build into the child's learning experiences which match the stage which he has reached in conceptual development.

Teachers of young children are particularly gifted in establishing sound emotional and social conditions in their classrooms. Those who fail to make good personal contact with children rarely stay in the job, and we are left with extremely sensitive people in charge of our young children. These teachers usually exercise great skill in handling children and many deal intuitively with problematic emotional and social situations. Even so, the teachers' knowledge of developmental patterns may be used to improve the child's opportunity to mature both socially and emotionally. He needs to meet challenge along with stability in his slow growth towards maturity, and what is expected of a child at each stage is geared to his individual pattern of social and emotional growth.

3

The same principles apply to the child's physical education. There is much more to movement than physical and psychological satisfaction. It is through his own movements that the child gains knowledge of his physical world, and early thinking grows out of the child's manipulative skills. Movement is basic to early learning. The mobility of the child determines the extent of his environment, of his opportunity to handle, to feel and to let his skin, eyes and ears tell him about the world outside himself. Growing up involves the child in ever deepening active experience, and each movement of his body should in some way contribute to his cognitive growth.

In every direction we come up against the fact that good provision to meet the child's growth needs is merely a starting point. What we do with what is provided and what we continue to do about it will determine the quality of the child's experience. In order that he should obtain what he needs from the pre-selected situations offered in school, we need to examine every situation and build into it the possibility for the child to learn progressively from it.

Few people ever reach their own limits, because too often they reach a required standard at which point their performance is satisfactory and no further demands are made. Every learning situation should contain a sequence of in-built incentives, so that as one goal is reached the way opens towards the next. At each stage in his growth towards maturity the individual becomes capable of further learning, and the wonderful adventure need never cease so long as challenge maintains purpose and interest is held.

Chapter 2

Applying developmental knowledge

In the traditional classroom, attainment was measured against a set of standards relating to a mythical norm, and the syllabus was dictated by these standards. The emphasis was on outer-direction and the success of the teacher was judged by her ability to make children measure up to prescribed standards.

In the modern classroom, the teacher has the opportunity to devise learning situations with emphasis on self-direction on the part of the child, and achievement is geared to maturation of the individual. The difference between directing a child through a sequence of prescribed activities and enabling him to find his own way through well-structured situations is at the core of revised practice.

Structuring the learning situation depends on the teacher's ability to apply developmental knowledge to the provision which she makes. Before she can do this she must be perfectly clear about the processes of development and about the conceptual patterns underlying the child's comprehension of each facet of his life and learning.

Development implies an unfolding of the organism through a series of orderly changes always advancing towards maturity.

Recurring change and progress are the chief characteristics of development. The unfolding may be uneven in pace, but it is always integrative. Each stage is affected by the one which precedes it and affects the one following, and each aspect of development affects all other aspects at every stage. In the early years these changes take place in rapid succession. Advancement is at its peak during the first four years of life. During the next two or three years the pace is still quick. Thereafter the pace slackens.

Knowledge of the child's growth patterns enables the teacher to know what to expect of the child, and to know how much or how little he needs in the way of challenge at each stage. Forcing him beyond his pace can prohibit further learning as effectively as withholding opportunity and challenge. The task for the teacher may seem overwhelming, but a firm grasp of the principles which apply to all developmental processes can reduce this formidable task to one which she can tackle successfully. Let us examine how this works out in practice.

When we are confronted by an unfamiliar word we refer to a dictionary for its meaning. The dictionary offers a definition of the term and fixes its meaning by relating it to other terms. If we know some of these terms we extract such meaning as is common to all of them and attach it to the unfamiliar term. That is, we fall back on earlier experience as a guide to a new situation.

Every concept dealt with in adult life has grown out of personal experience, and all the ideas we handle as adults have their roots in our earliest understanding. Adult concepts are the end product of life-long cognitive growth, and even the most abstract of our ideas had simple concrete beginnings.

Take, for example, the concept of space. The child has experience of space and some understanding of it long before the word 'space' holds any meaning. Before birth the child had experience of space as an enclosed place in which he was protected. Eventually he is ejected into a great outside space, but is totally unaware of its dimensions. His early exploratory movements help him to become aware of his own body, of where it stops and the outside world begins. He learns to know himself as a separate entity in space, but during his first months the child's perception of space is bound by what he can touch. As he becomes more mobile his space expands, but it remains, from his point of view, an enclosed area. The baby may be taken out for a ride in his pram and have personal contact with a vast amount of space, but what is beyond his reach doesn't exist and only gradually does he become aware that his egocentric world is not the whole of the universe. He sees the moon or the clouds and reaches out convinced that he can grasp them in much the same way as he grasps the woolly ball dangling from the canopy of his pram. Only gradually does the possibility of things beyond his reach dawn on him.

He learns to walk, to crawl and to run. He can move over great distances in space and still not reach its limits. There is a vast difference between the space of outdoors and the space of indoors, and while most children are familiar with expansive outdoor space, many enter school with no experience of large indoor space. When they are confronted with a large indoor space such as a school hall, they simply don't know what to do with it, and for a time either rush round madly, in an attempt to come to terms with it, or hide away in a corner because it frightens them.

By the time a child enters school he is aware of his position in space. He knows up and down, over and under, before and behind, and later perhaps above and beneath, and left and right. A space may be a hole, or a gap between himself and the next child, the part that keeps objects separated, or what is between shapes. Objects can be spaced out. A space can mean emptiness. There is also the notion of inside and outside which embraces the idea of enclosure.

The five- or six-year-old may perceive space as bound by a line which 'goes all the way round', and he draws a square in the same way as he draws a circle. The seven-year-old is beginning to relate his ideas of space to the concept of time, in the sense that space in time is the gap between events.

At the same time the child watches television programmes in which missiles are launched into deep space, and the word 'space ship' may mean the shape of the vessel, or the way in which it is propelled. He now realises that space is not bound by what he can touch, but he may still think of it as bound by the distance which the space ship can reach. Space is a place. He can 'find a space' for himself on the hall floor, or 'make a space' on the settee for his friend. He may be driven in a car by his father at great speed and still not reach the end of outside space. He may travel by plane to a holiday resort and discover with amazement that space is 'high up' as well as 'a long way off'. He knows that some objects are near while others are far away, or in other words that they hold a position in space.

The child of seven is not surprised when man lands on the moon, while Mars and Venus are just other places to visit. He may be eleven or twelve before he begins to comprehend space as that immeasurable expanse without closure in which earth and other planets are suspended.

In a similar way we could select any word or concept used by the adult and trace its evolutionary growth from the concrete situation in which the individual operates in an egocentric fashion, to the abstract notion which exists in the mind and which is available to all minds which reach out for it. Development always proceeds from the general to the specific, from a group of experiences which are seen to have something in common to the idea which is abstracted from these related experiences.

Explaining space to a child has no effect on his understanding until physical experience has laid a foundation of meaning. In the early stages it is through his body that he understands. Where an adequate range of experiences is provided, the child does the rest for himself, but if experience is withheld the emerging ideas are bound to suffer. A child might read a whole book about space, or listen to thousands of words telling him about space, but unless he has raced round a room, eased his head between railings, packed his toys into a cupboard, flung a ball high into the air and swung to and fro from a suspended rope, his understanding of those words will remain unawakened.

It is through the physical situation that the teacher can secure understanding for the young child. It isn't information that he needs, but the opportunity to formulate sound ideas and to learn how to make use of his ideas as they develop. At a later stage, information will help him to expand his own ideas, but only if those ideas are already there.

Armed with knowledge of the way in which the child's ideas about space develop, the adult can plan a sequence of experiences which match the child's unfolding ideas. In the early stages the child needs access to large indoor and outdoor spaces as well as to confined ones. He needs someone to discuss with him his experience of up and down, left and right, etc., and adequate play with objects which can be spaced out. He needs to explore all the ways in which he can move in space and to discover that out of doors he never reaches the limits of space. In short, the ordering of his experiences depends on what the adult provides, and there is no other means of ensuring that the child's concepts are soundly based.

Similar principles operate at every level and the introduction of a simple skill such as sewing illustrates the way in which the child may be helped to develop a skill through the design of the activity itself.

Knowing that the child must first explore the materials and tools in his own way before 'making something with them', we can set out attractive squares and oblongs of fabrics, such as thick soft cotton or firm wool, which are easy to sew, large-eyed needles ready threaded with smooth embroidery cotton and ready knotted. The incentive to experiment is one which few children can resist, and simple, good materials reward the child's first efforts with some success. He sews and later decides that he has 'made a mat', or simply 'done sewing'.

We added pins so that some attempt may be made to set a hem before sewing it. As confidence is gained we leave the child to cut his own shapes, thread his own needle and secure the end or tie his own knot. There is now a choice of threads and the range of materials is widened. He 'wants to make something' and we show him how to design a simple purse, to stitch a button and align it with a hole. We may suggest that 'the house corner needs new curtains' or 'a table cloth', and he has now to 'measure' his fabric and make his product fit.

Success breeds ambition, and larger pieces of material are made available for those who can use them economically. Simple patterns for making doll's clothes become part of the sewing corner, and the puzzling problem of how to cut back and front at the same time must be solved and tried out in newspaper before using precious fabric. Eventually a range of materials inspires the desire to make a T-shirt, or a tunic 'for the dressing up'. Meanwhile, the introduction of attractive embroidery threads suggests the use of 'decorations' or 'stitched pictures' to enhance basic designs.

Most teachers are skilful in planning progression in such simple concrete situations, and there is really little difference between structure at this level and when dealing with the development of skills and concepts at a higher level.

Chapter 3

Learning through discovery

Curiosity acts as the child's most powerful drive. From his first moments curiosity activates the child towards learning and plays an essential role in his survival. Through touching and handling he gains personal information about a great many things in his environment. What he finds out for himself is his for the first time and from his point of view is discovered. The evidence of his senses is the foundation of the child's understanding, and the classroom is organised and equipped in a way which encourages him to touch, see, hear, taste and smell as his main means of making sense of his world. Throughout his early years personal knowledge is all that he understands. Discovery learning is always based initially on first-hand experience. Finding out from books and from other people comes later and is grafted on to foundational understanding.

The teacher plays an essential role in the discovery approach. The material which she prepares sparks off interest and curiosity. She plans a sequence of stages through which the child strives towards the ultimate goal of abstract ideas. By sharing the child's exploratory adventures, her well-stocked and mature mind stirs the child's mind. Her active participation in what he is doing helps to sustain and channel his efforts so that his learning has depth and direction.

Amongst the materials and objects which are of greatest natural interest to the child are the simple materials which have fascinated man from primitive times. The crust of the earth and the canopy of atmosphere in which life is enfolded contain all the materials which challenged primitive man and gave him the opportunity to become intelligent. Soil and water and all that they contain are the child's first natural sources of exploration. Most teachers include these simple materials in their classroom equipment, but how often are they organised in a way which ensures vital learning?

The baby and the toddler live for much of their time very near to the ground, and to scrabble in the soil and dabble in the water are deep-seated needs in each individual. The soil contains many ingredients: sand and clay, rocks and stones, decayed vegetation and other materials which make up the soil itself, together with objects such as fossils and shells and living things such as plants and insects which use the soil as a temporary or permanent home. Soil in substantial quantities and clumps of turf are rarely seen in the classroom, and what we usually find are certain components of soil such as sand or clay, and sometimes rocks or stones, alongside 'water play'. We shall therefore begin by looking at ways in which learning by personal discovery from these materials may be improved.

Sand is usually present in a sand tray, that is in small quantities. Where the child has access to it in fairly substantial quantities, more will be discovered. One of the first things that children do with sand is to explore it with their hands, and dry sand offers more textural experiences than wet sand. Sensory exploration acquaints the child with its grittiness and its sifting qualities. It can be pushed, or blown about, patted or scattered. Sometimes it gives way easily, at others it is solidly resistant. At a certain stage in his growing knowledge of the material the child needs the help of an adult in crystallising his experiences and finding words to express his ideas, and such words as rough, smooth, gritty, hard, soft, sift, spray, etc., will acquire fresh meaning.

There are many kinds of sand, and different grades vary widely in both texture and colour. Miniature cars can be set to run down slopes made from sands of different grades, and friction can be related to texture. The introduction of different kinds of sand

11

takes the child a stage further in his observation. Silver sand from the river, golden sand from the sea shore, black coarse sand from volcanic islands, builder's sand and the whole range of coloured sands from Alum Bay speak to the child of their wide-ranging nature, and may stir his curiosity as to their origin. Sandstone may provide him with some clues, and a magnifying glass will help him to develop his ideas, but he may be six or seven before he has sufficient experience of the physics of the earth to understand the processes of weathering.

Sand can be poured, and the addition of such equipment as sieves, funnels, jugs and other vessels, tins with holes down the side or at the bottom, etc., enables the child to observe the way pouring sand behaves. 'Why does it sift from the funnel in the shape of a cone?' 'Why do the slopes vary according to the texture of the material?' 'Does sand fill up all the spaces?' The conservative nature of the material and the invariance of its behaviour are notions available to the child in these experiences.

At this stage, the child's knowledge of conservation, or his understanding of the idea that the amount of matter remains constant irrespective of the shape it takes or the way in which it is distributed or partitioned, begins to develop in relation to the concrete situation. Much depends on the selection of vessels for pouring, and care must be taken to include a range of containers which are equal in capacity while differing in shape, so as to ensure contact with these ideas.

Sand is 'heavy', but not all types of sand have the same weight by bulk. Equal measures of different sands can be balanced against one another, or compared with simple units such as dried peas, which enables the child to observe small differences in weight.

The introduction of a hair-dryer offers the opportunity for the child to observe the effects of wind on sandy areas and helps to establish ideas which he will later associate with what he learns about deserts and sandy places.

The addition of water modifies the behaviour of sand. Damp sand sticks together and clings to the skin. It can be moulded and it retains the impressions of fingers and objects. More water brings about a further change. Water drains through sand, which acts as a filter. When wet sand dries out it returns to its original condition, unlike sugar or salt which the child cannot retrieve once he has dissolved them in water.

The outdoor sand pit, containing large quantities of sand,

extends each of these experiences and adds others. Heaps of sand can be sculptured, used to build castles and moats, tunnels and bridges, ramps and mountains. Sweeping sand with a broom or a besom has an interesting effect, and a barrow laden with sand requires skilful handling.

Man uses sand in many ways and experience of sand on a large scale helps children to find answers to such questions as, 'Why is sand a poor foundation?'; 'What part does it play in building?'; 'Or in the construction of motorways?'; 'When are sandbags effective?'; 'Why is sand used to make dunes?'.

An egg timer or hour glass suggests other uses of sand. Sand also acts as a scouring agent and was at one time used to blot wet ink. In these and other of man's uses of sand the child may see how the properties which he has discovered have been employed.

Each fresh experience adds to the child's concept of sand. Moreover, at each stage in his cognitive development the child's understanding of a simple material increases, and it could never be said that 'the child of six has learned all he can about sand', or 'has grown out of it'. Man goes on learning about the natural materials which he uses throughout the whole span of his life.

Water is another popular classroom commodity. It is used for mixing paint, paste and pastry, for washing hands and floors, for drinking, and there may well be a 'water play' corner. The teacher may even provide vessels for pouring, lengths of tubing and a squeeze bottle. But too often water play is regarded as valuable mainly for its therapeutic properties. Children are left to dabble in it, when there is so much more to be learned from it.

The child discovers a great deal about water through his day-to-day contact with it. He probably has more opportunity to learn about water than about any other simple substance. His experience of water begins before birth. It is one of the first things that he meets after birth, and in fact accounts for a high percentage of his environment throughout life. Indeed, if he were dehydrated there would be little left of his physical body. The affinity between man and water is expressed in the fascination which it holds for him at every stage in his life.

There are, however, many properties of water which may remain unobserved by the child unless the adult builds into the child's environment the opportunity for him to discover them. Water, like sand, is usually available only in limited quantities in the classroom, and the child's discoveries will be severely restricted if his water experiments depend on meagre equipment and but a few pints of the wonderful stuff.

To take just one of its properties, the fact that water can be poured. The child needs to watch the way in which it fills all spaces in transparent containers, pushing out the air and staying level which ever way the container is tilted. Water can be poured from one vessel to another. Jars and tins of different sizes, and graded in size, will offer opportunity to observe its conservative nature. Among the vessels provided, a number of different shapes should contain the same amount of water when full, so that the child may discover the idea that, for example, 'these are all a pint, but they look different'. The young child may not believe the evidence of his senses, and may need to reach a later stage in cognitive development before he can accept this fact as constant, or grasp the idea that 'three of these little ones fill the big one'.

Water always pours downwards. Tins with holes down the side illustrate the effects of air pressure. The rate at which water empties from tins with one or more holes is related to air pressure. An air-tight tin with a hole in the lid and the base illustrates the principle of a valve. Unless the right equipment is available, these discoveries will not be made.

Although water pours downwards, it can be made to shoot upwards, and the introduction of a length of tubing with its ends inserted into the base of two tins, will enable the child to make a fountain.

Dissolving experiments require the addition of hot water and suitable soluble substances, together with some which will not dissolve. Salt and sugar, sand and flour, dried milk, cocoa, die, paint powder, paste, etc., provide a variety of experiences in mixing and dissolving from which the child may deduce some important principles.

Flotation is a fascinating source of enquiry. Different types of wood illustrate the wide variations in the floatability of wood. A milk-bottle top, opened out, floats, but when screwed up tight it sinks. In the right shape even plasticene can be made to float. Some objects will be difficult to classify and so open the way to fresh experimentation.

One group of children decided that 'only light things float'. The teacher asked them to find out whether all the things which floated could easily be blown about. This led the children to reconsider their first decision.

In a similar way, we can take each of the properties of water and plan a sequence of experiences leading to its full discovery. The child could be told these facts, and he may or may not retain them as facts. On the other hand, where the right equipment partners the opportunity to experiment with water in reasonably generous quantities, these properties are discernable to the child, and when he discovers them for himself they become personal to him.

We should also remember that the child of six or seven is beginning to show interest not only in what happens, but in why it happens. The concept of causality is not available to the child at this stage, but he is capable of finding out that one thing follows another and even of forming some hypothesis which may be tested. He knows, for instance, what to expect of water when he pours it and may be able to suggest other liquids which behave in a similar way. If he is given the opportunity to experiment with pouring liquids such as oil, glycerine, or bottled sauce, and to say what he can about the differences between the way they behave, he may draw some useful conclusions. What the child may discover for himself depends on what is available, and the teacher who is fully aware of the possibilities for discovery is in a position to know what to provide.

The quality of these experiences is vastly enhanced by the interest and participation of the teacher, and she should not feel guilty of 'taking time off' for this purpose from, for example, 'hearing children read'. From such experiences the child not only learns about the nature of the earth which supports him, but accumulates depth experiences to which his words may be attached. If the words which he learns to say and manipulate are to be understood and used, then their meaning must be made available to him. Sand, water and other natural materials need as much care and attention as library books and mathematical apparatus.

In some classrooms we find 'discovery' catered for by 'investigation' displays or tables and work cards. Let us therefore pause here for a moment and examine the function of work cards in the light of what we know about the way in which children learn.

The fact that children learn as individuals at their own pace makes nonsense of mass instruction, and the work card is a means of providing individual tuition. In using work cards the teacher decides the direction which the child shall take. She may break the course down into a series of small but ordered steps leading towards some specified goal; she may include open-ended problems which set the child searching and thinking; she may orientate the child towards some selected aspect of a study. Whatever technique she employs, she depends on the child's ability to interpret and comprehend the instructions on the card, and the more able he is to do this, the more effective her instructions become. She initiates the child's observation and study and directs it, albeit by remote control, and in so doing imposes structure on the learning situation from without.

Individualised learning and informality are often confused, and direction at an individual level is just as traditionally formal as class teaching. In certain circumstances the involvement of a whole class under the leadership of the teacher has a positive part to play in the modern classroom. A good example is the introduction of a fresh topic or theme such as the 'Happiness' theme illustrated in Chapter 5. We do not condemn class teaching, or even class instruction, but we should be clear about the difference between the child learning through teacher instruction and the child becoming the architect of his own learning.

Where sufficient attention has been paid to the content and design of a learning situation, the need for work cards disappears, and it is the situation itself which leads the child towards ever deepening comprehension, yet leaves him free to follow a direction which will bring him maximum benefit. With so many things in the world to be learned, why should the adult make the selection when in the end the child will have to work out his own destiny?

In a work card system the pre-reading child and the slow reader are severely hampered and may spend much of their time struggling to find out what it is the teacher wants them to do. Yet these same children are perfectly capable of learning what a well-structured situation can teach them. In many cases work cards become a barrier to learning as well as limiting it.

Freedom to learn does not mean leaving children rudderless in an environment which is merely filled with things to do. Even material of good quality may offer only limited scope if it is not well organised. Understanding the child and his cognitive growth is only the first step. The complementary step is to understand in depth each aspect of learning available to the child. The synthesis of the two results is well-structured and individually relevant learning, and this should be our aim in whatever the child is doing.

Chapter 4

The development of movement

Movement is inseparable from life. It is also inseparable from learning. The child's need for movement is virtually insatiable and his powers of movement generate much of his learning. There is a great deal more to movement than mere physical development.

The five-year-old who is expected to keep still may try to oblige, but only a lethargic child will do this for more than a few minutes. When we ask a five-year-old to sit still we make him feel inadequate, because we are asking him to do what he is not able to do well and finds extremely difficult to do at all.

Every aspect of learning involves the child in some kind of movement, and even thinking—or movement of the mind—originates in movement at a physical level. Where movement opportunities are inadequate, learning remains at a premium, and even the most intelligent child will not realise his gifts if his movement development is inadequately catered for.

The child uses movement as an aid to satisfying his personal needs. Movement gives him great pleasure and plays an essential role in social contact. It is through his own actions that a child becomes aware of himself as a separate entity. The child uses bodily movement as a means of expressing and recording impressions and reactions. Movement is an ever ready medium through which the child can find a creative outlet. Most important of all, the child moves in order to explore a world which in his early years extends for him only as far as he can reach.

In the earliest stages of life involuntary movement and intentional movement are fused. Movement of the whole body precedes movement of isolated parts of it, and many five-year-olds do not have the control required to move a single part of the body while keeping the rest still. Control of the body to the point of keeping it still may not be achieved before the age of seven. Growing bodily control brings growing confidence in the body, and the child of nine who can make his body obey his will is a major achievement in any educational system.

A child growing up in a tropical paradise has no need for physical education; his environment provides it for him. But we bring up our children in confined indoor and outdoor spaces which are full of restrictions and dangers. In school we provide substitutes for the challenge of trees and rivers and rocky mountains in the form of dance, apparatus and games, and the adult is then faced with the problem of when to leave the child free in his movement exploration, when to give him specific tuition, and when to introduce practice. A major job of the teacher is to help the child to grow more aware of his body and of the quality of any movements that he makes. By doing so, she will contribute to his learning in a great many ways.

Some teachers of five-year-old children seem afraid to leave them free in a hall or on a field to tumble about at will. 'If I let them go they get wild and out of control,' one teacher explained, 'and they won't settle down back in the classroom.'

Every normal child of five is capable of moving in a great many ways, and when we leave him free he will show us the movements in which he is most skilled. We can learn a lot about where to make a start in the child's movement education when we observe the kinds of movements he makes when 'turned loose' in an adequate space. One child races round and round the room screaming until he drops to the ground exhausted. Another rolls about on the floor, or lies on his back kicking his legs in the air. A third tries to balance on his hands kicking his legs up behind, while his neighbour bounces about on his bottom. Yet another jumps on and off any object she can find. Each of them is concerned with his own movements and shows little interest in

19

sharing movement with another child. Each tries out all that his body can do and seldom tries to imitate another's movements.

Five-year-old children are at the scribble stage in their movement development and need time to discover their individual possibilities before beginning to modify them. They need to build up adequate relationships between themselves, the ground and the spaces in which they are able to move, before turning their attention to moving in more specified ways.

At the scribble stage in movement development the child is doing much more than simply exploring the ways in which his body can operate. Amongst other things, he is accumulating his first impressions of space, direction and movement qualities, from which mathematical and scientific ideas will grow.

Movement education begins when the teacher extends basic movement experiences such as running and walking, climbing and balancing, jumping and skipping, rolling and crawling, and encourages experiments in combining movements. Movement awareness need not be restricted to a particular period in the day. At all times, when the children are moving about the classroom or school, building with bricks and blocks, manipulating equipment, or getting dressed and undressed, opportunities for improving and extending movement skills present themselves for the teacher and child to use.

Once children have a good basic movement vocabulary and are beginning to acquire skill in moving parts of the body, the teacher can then introduce simple equipment to add further challenge to the situation. Very often the hall or playground is equipped with climbing apparatus, and because the use of it is timetabled teachers feel obliged to use it as part of the movement lesson. Thoughtful observation of the way in which children move, particularly in a hall where they may be experiencing a large indoor space for the first time, leads one to suppose that stimulating equipment should be introduced as and when it is needed, and that individual small apparatus is often more appropriate in making a start.

Balls of different sizes and weights make a suitable introduction to the use of apparatus. Not all young children handle a ball happily, and some need to kick a big one about for quite a long time before beginning to play with one which they can catch and bounce. Beanbags, objects to jump over or jump from, and something on which to balance (just a plank on the floor is enough for some children) will help to extend children's knowledge of what they can do.

At this stage the child's movements aren't easily classified into agility skills, dance, games and the like, and most children need plenty of time to explore movement in an undifferentiated way before more classified forms of activity are introduced. Many children will be six or seven before they are ready to participate in specialised physical work.

Chronological age is obviously a meagre guide to the child's movement development and this complicates the situation when dealing with large groups. In schools where the classes are mixed in chronological age, the range of movement between individual children is probably wider than in any other aspect of their development. In open-plan schools children may have access to open spaces at any point in the day. Where movement opportunities are timetabled, space should be set aside for free experimentation by the less mature. Climbing apparatus and other equipment make an important contribution to physical education, but many children have urgent physical jobs to do before they can benefit from the use of apparatus, and very few are ready when first entering school to work together in a large group. The youngest children have much to do in developing their personal basic movements and establishing their individual rhythms before they are ready to share movement with another child, or with a group of children. Many can move very well, but co-operating with the teacher and following her suggestions may need to wait until they are confident in moving as individuals amongst a lot of other children.

The tiny child is intensely interested in his own body. It is one of his earliest discoveries, and entry into school increases his need to identify his individual body as unique among the many other bodies which he finds there. Some children may need to identify and name parts of the body and learn the vocabulary of movement instruction. A child of five may know head, arm and leg, but not shoulder, elbow and ankle, and he may be quite at a loss if told to hop or skip. It isn't that he can't do these things, he simply doesn't understand what is required of him, and a comprehensive body topic is a very helpful and profitable study for the four- and five-year-olds.

Even the six-year-old, who may be quite skilful with a ball or rope, may have great difficulty in relating his skill to a partner.

21

Once children gravitate towards apparatus they need time to consolidate their relationship with it before being expected to partner others and to participate in games. The child of seven may enjoy a ball game with a small group of friends, but the rules are devised as the game proceeds, and rarely in the first school are children ready to operate rules laid down in a book.

Young children who are still at the stage when speech is halting and even a barrier to what they wish to express use movements of the body and face as their most articulate forms of communication. Peter stamps in frustration when the string of his pull-along toy gets entangled with its wheels. Thomas jumps up and down at the excitement of seeing his Dad walking up the drive. Sue rocks blissfully to and fro nursing her new dolly. Nicholas spins round and round like a top until he drops exhausted as he waits for Mum to pack their picnic in readiness for a day at the sea.

These expressive movements are the raw material of drama, mime and dance. They capture a mood and convey an impression of the way in which a child is reacting to a situation which stirs him. The watchful teacher can build up a small library of such movements and can later weave them into patterns of dance by reminding the child of the experience which gave rise to them. In other words, she uses the simple bodily material which the child brings with him on entering school as the basis of more organised movement patterns. These patterns are built around the child's spontaneous movement forms, and are not a means of making the child's body translate the teacher's theme or idea.

When the child is fully conversant with what his body can do and with the ways in which it can serve him, he is then able to start using it in ways prescribed by others. The teacher's suggestions then become a challenge and point the way to extending his skills. As his skill develops, the child needs to reach his own limits, and the challenge of others has an important part to play. Introduced too soon, the suggestions made by the teacher and the challenge of sharing movement experience with others may restrict the child in his discovery of his natural movement forms.

The skill of the teacher involves knowing how long to hold back and allow the child to explore and discover, when to encourage him to repeat what he has discovered, when to stimulate him to extend his initial movement experiences and then to modify them or share them with other children, and finally when to practise skills in order to improve them.

Virtually all that the child learns is based on movement of some kind, and reference will be made in subsequent chapters to the significance of movement development in every aspect of the child's work. Teachers who wish to extend their knowledge of movement experience in school will find that *Movement in the Primary School* (H.M.S.O., 1972) is helpful.

Chapter 5

Developmental drama

There was a time when drama in the infant school was indulged in mainly as a means of providing entertainment for parents while perhaps making a minor contribution to the development of speech. Today it finds a place in most classrooms, yet few teachers fully acknowledge the contribution of drama to the all-round development of the child. Still fewer plan the child's drama education along developmental lines. Yet drama is an integral part of the young child's life and it merits the same care and attention as is paid to all his other communication skills.

When we watch young children at play we are left in no doubt about their interest in drama. From a very early age, drama in one of its many forms is a very popular natural play form. We could go so far as to say that it is essential to the personal development of the child. Indeed the child uses drama for his own purposes as a means of finding out about himself, about other people and about the world around him. He is less concerned about an audience, and the idea of a finished production for the benefit of a formal audience is far removed from the child's uses of drama during his early years. Considering the role of drama in classical education, it seems surprising that today it is frequently undervalued, and an objective study of the part played by dramatic experience in the child's development has yet to be made.

Drama is essentially concerned with people and with interaction between them. It is also concerned with symbolism and interpretation, and is one of many modes of communication available to the child on entering school. The contribution made by the teacher should be based on the child's spontaneous dramatic play, and a beginning can be made by studying the child's free expressive play. When do children dramatise? Where does much of it take place? What inspires it? What purpose does it serve? Is there anything the teacher can do to make it more profitable to the child?

A prime aim in education is to help the child to become articulate. Although the varied use of words is highly important in this respect, this is only one of many forms of communication. Many of our children are verbally inarticulate, but all of them can move, use facial expression and gesture, cry or laugh, make marks on surfaces and handle materials; in short, they have at their disposal many ways of expressing a personal view of experience, and each can be articulate in some particular way. The child's concepts of communication are established and then developed by helping him to use the means of saying what he wishes to say that comes most naturally to him.

Children turn to drama as a means of exploring the personalities of other people, or of finding out more about themselves by playing out some situation. This is a very adequate means of discovering how people live, and through watching children we soon get to know how they feel about their mother and father, their teacher, the refuse collector and the visiting inspector. Much of this play starts in the house corner and is inspired by people who interest the child, but objects which symbolise some person or situation, e.g. a policeman's helmet, crown, wig, hat, flowing cloak, etc., are equally stimulating.

Younger children rely very much on bodily movement, embroidered by mime and gesture, and a whole sequence of events may be played out without a word being spoken. Their drama is frequently a free-for-all, with several heroes and one unwilling victim. Hospital play, for instance, usually includes an abundance of nurses and doctors with but a single patient. In the course of a few minutes roles may be changed, and the unwilling patient suddenly gains supremacy as a doctor. Words may be added to make the position clear: 'You've broken your leg and you can't walk. We have to make a bed thing on poles to carry you . . .'

The supreme confidence of children in free dramatic play is quite remarkable. The only rules they know are those which they themselves have created. They know how the doctor performs an operation, because they have formed and use their own impressions of his actions. They act as they think and find out what it is like to be a doctor by being one for a time. Identification comes easily to the young child. For the time being he isn't playing at being someone else, he *is* that other person. Such dramatic skill is well developed from the age of three or four, and when the child enters school we do well to use his skill rather than to try and introduce drama forms of our own.

What can the teacher do to improve the quality of the child's natural drama forms? She can provide suitable properties and dressing-up equipment. She can enrich the child's experience of the world. She can feed in ideas from stories, pictures, poetry and the creative work of the masters. She can extend and enrich the child's vocabulary of movement and speech. Most important of all, she can provide the kind of atmosphere which is conducive to uninhibited communication. In short, she can ensure the quality of the materials from which he creates his drama, but in the early stages she leaves the form his drama takes to him. As the child becomes more articulate, she can suggest more challenging topics, provoke thought and imagination by introducing some definite form for the communal act of presentation, and provide the intellectual activity of working out a dramatic pattern which is to be repeated. Young children rarely need an audience, but the child of seven or eight begins to enjoy the interaction between players and onlookers. Occasionally, parents and other adults can be called in to participate, but the idea of parent audiences at this stage comes from the teacher, not the child.

Good material for house play does not necessitate elaborate furniture and utensils. Small sizes of real pottery and culinary ware, with very simple furniture, leave more to the child's imagination than miniature stoves with realistic knobs. As far as possible, children should make their own curtains, cloths, pictures, rugs, etc. The house corner should be respected and ordered, not a fringe activity or a place in which small boys establish a fort. Dressing-up materials should be kept nearby, thrown over a rail perhaps, and always available: a stethoscope, a nurse's apron and cap, odds and ends of uniform, almost any familiar object used by people whom the child is likely to meet, together with boxes, bricks, blocks and the like from which children can construct a shop, fire station, castle, or other simple setting for extended dramatic play.

Exciting experiences for children are often quite simple ones. An expedition to the local post-office or bakery is just as stimulating to a five-year-old as a flight to Mexico. Encouraging the children to ask questions, talk to people, observe with care and think about their experiences will improve their impressions. Well-chosen stories and poems provide images for creative thinking and words for the child's vocabulary. Listening when children do try to communicate their impressions in words is often of greater value than telling them what to think and see.

The teacher who encourages children to be themselves because she accepts and appreciates them will establish an atmosphere in which children can express their reactions and impressions with confidence. In such an atmosphere drama will fill its correct function.

By the time he is six, the child has accumulated considerable experience of human behaviour. He has a well-established idea of himself, and is becoming conscious of his own feelings and aware of the feelings of others. Mime demands a concentrated effort to observe the behaviour of others, and to summon and use a wide variety of feelings. The six-year-old is capable of making this effort, and through mime he can be called upon to translate precisely the behaviour of others and to express his own powers of feeling. In order to do this the child must transport himself into the situation and concentrate on the action involved. In mime he is expected to present his interpretation through movement, gesture and facial expression, rather than through words, and it is therefore a good starting point for introducing more definite form into dramatic play.

Secrets and surprises always excite young children, and a simple start can be made by using a box. To begin with, an actual box is used, but as the children gain confidence in their ideas the box can be dispensed with.

There are many variations on the same theme. For example, it is Christmas time and the box is huge, wrapped in gay paper and tied with an enormous bow. The child knows exactly what he wants for a present. On discovering that the box is for him, he becomes very excited. He lifts it, shakes it, listens, trying to decide whether it contains what he most desires. He is told that he can open the box and he can scarcely wait to get inside. He unwraps it and lifts the lid, but the box doesn't contain what he wanted, only a toy which he already possesses.

The core idea of this mime is a dramatic change of feeling, and the child is expected to emphasise the difference between excitement and pleasurable anticipation, and intense disappointment. At this age the child can express contrast in feelings, but may be unable to dramatise finer shades of feeling, and further ideas should be developed round the theme of dramatic changes in emotion.

Further ingredients may be added to the basic theme. For example, the box is discovered on the top shelf in mother's wardrobe. Christmas Day is three days away and there is no label on the box to indicate who it is for. Alternatively, there are two boxes similar in shape and size, and the labels have got mixed up. Or the box could be buried treasure, an Indian ring box containing a magic ring, the tiniest box in the world containing a 'Great Secret Thing', or a packing case containing sections which fit together to make a new play house.

The six-year-old has very varied tastes and interests, and while the box theme should relate generally to personal experience, there should be opportunity for the more intelligent child through the introduction of more imaginative ideas.

A rather more developed theme, offering scope for as many children in the class as wish to participate, could start with the idea of a picnic. This could involve dressing up to indicate the characters of mother, father, grandmother, children, etc. Each child suggests—by miming—who he is supposed to be and what he is doing in the way of preparation for the picnic, making sandwiches, collecting bathing trunks, beach wear, fishing tackle, etc. At the last minute a message is received by telegram, phone, or in person, bringing news which necessitates a change of plan.

On another occasion, the party could reach the picnic site. Some paddle or swim, others build sand castles or fish, others gather pretty shells or search for birds' eggs, shrimps and sea-urchins. The Punch and Judy Show attracts a crowd, and later everybody buys ice cream or rides on a donkey. At the height of the fun thunder is heard in the distance and lightning pierces the threatening clouds. Eventually, a bedraggled and dejected party gather their soggy possessions and make for home.

This type of mime may be repeated time and time again, adding fresh ingredients suggested by the children. It may eventually take on a more permanent form, or a series of episodes may emerge to be repeated at will. It can take place in the classroom, but if a large open space can be found, so much the better.

As the children gain confidence, the teacher should try to improve their powers of observation and interpretation. 'Grandma may be much older than you are, but is she really bent double when she walks?' 'How can you show that you are a father? When you all go out in the car, what does father do to make sure you drive along the right road?' 'Is that a castle you're building? How can you show that it isn't just a pie?'

Children don't always react as we expect, and the suggestion 'You look glum, Robert. Would you really look like that when Mother is packing sandwiches?' may earn the reply, 'But I don't like picnics. I like to spread jam out of a pot and it all gets runny at picnics.'

Once children have the idea of developing these simple themes, they should be encouraged to suggest their own themes and the ingredients from which to create incidents. These may arise from local events, or a visit. Fairs, bonfires, parties, expeditions to a shop or park, etc., are often more profitable starting points than the more abstract ideas which emerge from stories. Television is, of course, a powerful influence, and the teacher should be familiar with popular children's programmes. Animated objects and puppets are usually favoured and programmes built around them often provide some useful ideas.

The older child, who has had plenty of experience of free dramatic play and miming, is capable of handling a more clearly defined drama form. He can be called upon to study prescribed characters in some interesting situation and then to present his own interpretation of the story. The teacher's contribution lies in helping the children to select a suitable story, ballad or poem, and then to provide experiences which will enable the child to get inside the character which he is endeavouring to portray.

A popular library book at the moment is *The King's Hiccups* by John Randle (a 'Beginning to Read' book, Ernest Benn, 1971 and Gleichenhaus & Co, New York), and this will serve as an example of the way in which a story book may be used to stimulate dramatic expression. The story is humorous and simple. The King has hiccups, which is a distressing complaint for a King when he meets important people. The Prime Minister, the General and the Doctor try in vain to cure him. Then an insignificant little man with a big smile, who makes everyone laugh, succeeds. The book is colourful and attractively illustrated.

Pageantry has a universal appeal, and the wide variety of characters in the story provides scope for each child in the class. First the children decide who shall play each part, then each child makes some item of dress to depict his chosen character. The illustrations will help, and these often serve as a starting point for discussion which gives the teacher an opportunity to fill in the child's background knowledge. 'How do you know which one is the Prime Minister? Why does he wear a chain? What else is there about his clothing which makes him look important? Why is the Prime Minister one of the most important men in the country?' (Be ready for some interesting suggestions.)

The child who has fitted his crown, embroidered it with 'fruit-gum' jewels and sprayed it with gold paint, must put it on. The moment he puts on his crown he becomes someone else, but he may have much to learn before he becomes a king. 'Why did the King start work straight after breakfast? What sort of work does he do? We have a Queen. Tell me some of the things you have seen her doing on television. Look through all those newspapers and cut out any pictures of the Queen. What kind of person is she? We can make a list of all the words which tell us what she is like (kind, proud, good, fair, gracious, etc.). Why did the King feel so uncomfortable when he said "Hic" instead of "Good morning" to the Prime Minister?'

As the children begin to understand their various roles they can try out appropriate actions. For example, the King wakes up and finds he has hiccups. He receives the Prime Minister. He visits the army. He goes for a walk in the park and listens to the band. He stands on his head and holds his breath, rides a horse backwards, takes a pill.

Several children can try out a particular role before a decision is made. When the characters have been allocated, time can be allowed for further experiment before beginning to bring the characters together. Each child should know his character well before the characters are brought into contact with one another. The children can then try out some of the incidents, at first in mime and then adding such dialogue as they think fit. As much as possible should be conveyed through mime, and words are added only to clarify action.

Up to this point, the action has taken place in any available corner. Once the various incidents have been worked out in small groups, the story should be read to the children to remind them of the sequence. The action will then need to be transferred to a larger space such as the hall, field or playground, or even along an open corridor, allowing plenty of room for the whole class to become involved. When the sequence becomes familiar, the children will begin to elaborate the events, add incidents of their own and generally take over the story, or, using the same characters, create a new story.

Once the children can handle such simple stories with confidence, they can be introduced to more imaginative themes. Another popular book with this age group is *Indian Two Feet and his Horse* by Margaret Friskey (Muller, 1971, and Children's Press, Chicago), and this story provides a more ambitious canvas on which the children can work. Two Feet is a little Red Indian boy who longs for a horse. His father tells him, 'You must think like a horse to find one. Go find one.' After several fruitless attempts, Two Feet decides, 'If I were a horse, I would find a cool, cool spot.' He finds a cool spot, and a horse with a sore foot finds him. He is kind to the horse, who stays with him. Two Feet has a horse.

The children could first make Indian headdresses, 'leather' trousers and 'deer-skin' wraps, and perhaps an Indian tent. They could make mouth music, do Indian dances and songs, draw pictures on rock with pieces of bone, mime riding on a log, swinging from a tree, swimming across a river, etc., or create stories to tell around the camp fire at night. They will need to understand why having a horse was so important to Two Feet. Imagination needs facts on which to work, and geographical information about the background to the story would help to establish an authentic atmosphere.

The children could then focus on the leading characters, Two Feet, his father and the horse. Two Feet walks to the woods, to the river and climbs a hill. He rides down the hill on a rock and crosses the river on a log. He searches everywhere for his horse. His wise father offers advice. The children must decide whether to make a horse, mime one, or let a child play the horse's part.

31

The action takes place over a vast expanse of countryside, and Two Feet's journey calls for imaginative interpretation. This form of drama can involve the children in art work, dance, musical composition, story-telling and singing. Indeed, many aspects of learning can spring from the communication of ideas inspired by such a story.

This type of material, however, is only suitable for children whose drama experience is developed, and it should not be introduced until they are ready for it. Introduced too soon, it could rapidly deteriorate into a 'Red Indian shoot-up'.

The development of drama in schools has another very important function. It has always served as a useful link between the school and the outside world, particularly at times such as Christmas, when parents and visitors look to the school to celebrate the season by staging festivities in which both children and adults can join.

Teachers of young children today recognise that formal public performances are not in harmony with the nature of the child, and Christmas Concerts and Nativity Plays have virtually disappeared. Yet there are benefits to the school community from some form of public celebration, with its in-built social opportunity, and many teachers search for the kind of function which serves this purpose and yet fits into the way in which they are working. In schools built on open-plan lines, or where children are vertically grouped, or where there is free exchange between teachers, working as a team rather than as separate individuals, there may be additional problems.

What is called for is a form of festivity which involves as many members of the community as possible and which is in keeping with what we believe about the education of the young. As adults we need to take the lead, yet keep the children at the core, and the festivity should involve children at the creative level. That is, the celebration should grow from, and develop around, the ideas of the children themselves. It should take the form of a partnership between adults and children. It should be flexible enough to accommodate itself to any type of school building, or mode of organisation. It should have form without being formal. It should encourage a high degree of spontaneity, avoiding any possibility of resulting in a child performance for the benefit of an adult audience.

One possibility is to take the idea of 'Happiness' as a starting point. The following suggestions may serve as a model to indicate the way in which similar themes could be used to meet the needs of different communities and different occasions.

Using poems, stories, music, pictures, etc., the 'Happiness' theme could be introduced by individual teachers to their own class groups. The children should be encouraged to express their own ideas of 'Happiness', which are then recorded by the teacher. Children of different ages in one school expressed the following personal impressions.

5 years   Happy is a birthday cake.

6 years   It's something exciting like a party, or the new baby.

7 years   It's winning at marbles. *(boys)*
            Making jokes and laughing at them.
            Having a lot of money to spend.

7 + years   Happiness is when I feel good; when it's all right. *(girls)*
            When you like people. *(girls)*

The teachers should also express and record their personal views of happiness.

When dealing with abstract themes, it is important to remember that a child's ideas vary a great deal according to the stage reached in cognitive development, and we should guard against imposing adult interpretations of the way in which the child's ideas are expressed. The four- and five-year-old child, for example, simply is what he feels, and he may have little in the way of an idea to express. If asked what 'happiness' means, he will either ignore the question, or divert the questioner. The six-year-old tends to 'think' of happiness as something which happens to him and can understand it only by relating it to a personal event. He may not really understand happiness as something which happens to others. The seven- and eight-year-old is beginning to view happiness as an experience to be shared, and even to understand it as a state of mind which can be evoked by him for others. The adult view of happiness is a state of well-being frequently develop- ing as a by-product of human relations. By blending the ideas of children and adults, each child is given access to a means of extending and developing his own ideas.

The next stage is to discuss ways in which these various ideas can be expressed and communicated. Movement and mime are suitable vehicles for the idea of a party, making a birthday cake, or receiving the new baby. Older boys are often difficult to involve, and they could be set to work assembling jokes, jingles, puns, riddles, etc., adding a few home-made ones, and dialogue suggests itself as a fitting way of sharing them with others.

The idea of 'feeling good' could be associated with music. Records used in Assembly, for example, are often firm favourites. Children could make their own selection and add discreet accompaniment with the aid of percussion. Original musical composition, or home-made songs based on 'happy' things, could be played on simple instruments, some of which could be made by the children.

Teachers could add their own choice of songs, or instrumental music, as a means of contributing their ideas of happiness. Parents could also be involved in this way, as could any interested member of the auxiliary staff. In one school the caretaker, who was a pianist, was invited to accompany carols sung by groups of parents. In his own words, 'It made my Christmas'.

These various activities could work towards a collective occasion or 'Festival of Happiness'. The school community acts both as audience and performers, and action could take place 'round the tree' in a hall or suitable area of an open-plan school. It may be possible to include some use of outdoor space, introducing a note of 'in-and-outness' to the celebration. The whole could reach a climax in something colourful such as a 'Rainbow Dance', using lengths of filmy coloured material and the children's spontaneous movements.

In a festival such as this everyone contributes and participates, offering what he can to the occasion and building around the idea of 'childhood happiness', which is in truth at the heart of the Christmas festival. The flexible nature of this approach enables any mode of communication to be employed, and each occasion will be unique, evolving from the children's versatile ideas.

There are always a few children who find difficulty in participating in an overt way, but who may be happy to contribute by helping to prepare the setting, dress the tree, make notices, send invitations, or help with simple props and costumes. The emphasis is on encouraging children to experience happiness and to learn to share it, rather than on building up tensions by 'putting on a show'.

In the days when the annual Christmas concert was regarded as being essential, much time and energy was lost to children and teachers in preparing and practising for the performance, and a vast sigh of relief followed afterwards. When we approach the occasion through the understanding of children, those who participate emerge refreshed rather than exhausted.

These principles could, of course, apply to other festive occasions such as an Eastertime Spring Festival, an Autumn Thanksgiving, or even the Official Opening of a school. Like other aspects of development, the child's interest and skill in drama goes through a sequence of stages, and much depends on the skill of the teacher in selecting material to match the stage of development reached by the child.

Chapter 6

Communication concepts

Communication is the art of sharing experience. It takes many forms, ranging from bodily movement and facial expression to talking and telepathy. In any of its various forms, it has three main ingredients: experience which gives rise to the need for exchange between individuals; an appropriate vehicle of expressions; and suitable symbols to represent what is to be conveyed. The sole purpose in developing communication skills is to use them, and the child's ability to handle symbols of all kinds depends on the development of sound ideas about communication.

The modern classroom provides the child with a lot to do, out of which grows his need to express impressions and then to exchange them with other people. It also provides many vehicles of expression in the shape of dramatic play, mime and dance, malleable materials and marking tools. It surrounds him with symbols which he already knows, and introduces him to new ones. Great emphasis is placed on the child's use of symbols, particularly literal and numerical ones. In a literate and numerate society the child needs to advance his skills in dealing with words and numbers, but we defeat our purpose if we encourage him to do so at the expense of other communication skills and concepts.

The quality of life in the classroom is what determines the quality of impressions which promote communication, and our first responsibility is to ensure that what the child does is worth doing. The main purpose of this book is to guarantee that each activity offers the child experience as opposed to merely 'doing', and a constant job of the teacher is to scrutinise each learning situation with a view to improving it. No part of the child's life is trivial and all his learning experiences merit the same attention.

As adults we are so accustomed to handling symbols that we virtually take them for granted and may be inclined to forget that many which are familiar to us are unexplored mysteries to the child. What is done about symbols in school needs careful examination, for unless the child really understands them and their purpose, he will never learn what is to be done with them. There is a vast difference between recognising symbols and using them, and knowing symbols is not the same as understanding them.

We do well to bring into the classroom the full range of symbols with which the child is familiar. From his earliest days, visible and audible symbols play a significant role in the child's life. By the time he is five he knows visible symbols such as arrows, road signs, advertising signs, notes, numbers, words, letters, maps, diagrams, pictures and toys, together with sound symbols such as buzzers, bells, whistles, clappers and hooters. In his pre-school days he plays with many of these in an exploratory way and gradually begins to understand that the symbols stand for not only present objects, but also absent objects. The sound 'doll', for example, represents the doll seen in the shop the other day and the doll which can be touched. Many children on entering school are able to interpret a wide variety of symbols; they can, that is, associate a symbol with some previous experience. A child may, for example, retain a sensory image of a petrol symbol and when he sees the sign later, even in two-dimensional form on paper, he can relate it to his own image.

The child's ability to produce and interpret symbols follows a well-ordered pattern which coincides with the development of his thought processes. In handling symbols he will first learn to discriminate, that is to perceive likenesses and differences between various types of symbols and between symbols of a similar order. The ability to discriminate leads to the ability to classify, or sort out symbols into their various categories. Later he will begin to understand the importance of their invariant nature and of the way in which they are ordered. Finally, and not before his thoughts are reversible, he will be able to deal with the analysis and synthesis of symbols and especially of word symbols.

Before entering the school the child has begun to observe differences between familiar symbols. He knows, for instance, that an arrow tells him which way to go, while the word patterns tell him what's inside the packet and notes are the symbols which tell him to sing. Observing differences leads naturally to observing similarities, and once the child can perceive similarities he can begin to classify. Most children of five can discriminate between words, number, musical notes, etc., and can sort them into their separate categories.

Discrimination and classification within a single category are more demanding. Most five-year-olds know that word and letter patterns together form one category of symbols, and we can begin by helping the child to see differences and similarities between them, and later to sort out, for example, long words and short words, those which begin or end in the same way, those with a certain shape in the middle, those which fit into a rectangle, those with tails, etc. He can at the same time learn to recognise the differences and similarities between the sounds attached to the letters and words. Some children have more confidence in dealing with visible classification than with auditory discrimination, but skill in each is essential to the child's literary development.

Fundamental to our use of symbols is their invariant nature. We may not switch around a 'p' or a 'd', nor turn a 'w' upside down, but we may vary slightly the shape of a letter without changing its significance. Variants of 'a', for example, all hold the same meaning. Many of these skills can be acquired by the child during the process of sharing a book or a story with an adult. The adults should let the child see how he sets about the problem of interpreting the patterns, and discussion with the child as he sees letters and words in action provides him with useful clues.

The next stage involves the child in learning the significance of order. Words and letters must be used in a prescribed order, and any change in order alters meaning. The use of *Breakthrough to Literacy* (Longman, for the Schools Council, and Bowmar, USA), or similar material, will help the child to see that 'Pat kicked the ball' is not the same as 'The ball kicked Pat', and that 'was' is not the same as 'saw'. Moreover, we order from left to right, and this mode of ordering dictates the way in which words appear on a page and the way in which the pages of a book are turned. There is nothing natural about this order, and the child learns about order in reading by having his attention drawn to it, as he learns to use the patterns himself.

The ability to analyse and synthesise, to break down or take apart and reassemble, emerges as the child enters the next stage in cognitive development. Not all children reach this stage in the infant school, for not until their thoughts are reversible can they deal with the skills employed in phonic analysis. Phonic skills are both auditory and visual, and as far as the majority of children are concerned, this stage must carry over into the junior school. The fact that a child has been told 'a dozen times' that c-a-t 'says cat' doesn't mean he knows it, although he may make an inspired guess and say 'pussy'.

The development of these ideas about symbolism and interpretation needs to take place within the context of the vehicle of expression. The child's ideas of words and letters, for instance, grow out of sharing print and making his own efforts to produce and understand it. Little is gained by dealing with symbols as an isolated skill until a later stage, when its function in the total reading process is understood.

At the same time, the child's concept of vehicles of expression needs attention. He brings with him into school many ways of expressing his impressions through dramatic play, movement, mime and gesture, laughing and crying, singing and shouting, handling malleable materials and making marks on paper. Few children in their early days of schooling are completely confident in making marks on paper. Many lack confidence in themselves and are extremely timorous about making symbols of a permanent nature. All of them need to develop the use of the medium or vehicle in which they are articulate if they are to form sound ideas about the processes of recording and exchanging impressions. Basic communication skills are learned through bodily movement or creative media, just as readily as, and sometimes more than, through using words and numbers.

The child's most natural vehicle of expression is his own body, and the use of it as a whole precedes the restricted use of parts of it such as the hands. The child has a personal vocabulary of spontaneous movements. These are interlaced with the imitation of movements observed in others, and it is with this vocabulary that most children begin to put into visible and audible form their impressions of experience. Watching the child as he plays freely may reveal more about the effects of experience than through any other form of expression.

During his first year in school the child may be more concerned about communicating with himself than with others. He records, in drama, creative work, gesture, exclamation, etc., his embryonic reactions. In this way he explores experience and converts it into a form which he can understand, and it thereby becomes more real to him and takes on more definite and permanent form. At some point his teacher, or some other person, responds to his attempts, and he begins to sense the pleasure of extending and deepening an experience by sharing it with others. Gradually the teacher fosters this point of view, encouraging the child to improve his techniques, for example by observing carefully and recording accurately, so that he may convey his impressions with every increasing precision.

The teacher also provides the child with opportunities to receive the impressions of others. She tells him stories, encourages other children to tell him about their experiences, plays records for him to listen to, shows him paintings and pottery and sculpture, and by encouraging him to respond to these experiences, helps him to understand the reciprocal nature of communication.

These principles apply to every mode of communication available to the child, and it is only when he has considerable skill and understanding of communication skills that the teacher begins to single out the child's use of marks on paper. Even then, in the early stages, pictorial representation is paid as much respect as literal and numerical signals.

The present-day explosion of knowledge has generated frenzied efforts to ensure its safe transmission to subsequent generations, and there is a conspiracy abroad to hasten the child's growth towards the use of symbols and in particular literal and numerical ones. Naturally, in a literate society the responsible adult must make the development of literacy and numeracy skills a major concern. The processes of communication, however, are as slow-growing as people themselves. Undue acceleration produces superficial skills, and if in the end a child is to understand symbols and find in them a useful means of personal communication, he must be given adequate time in which to come to terms with them. We have ample evidence from research into intensive language programmes, for instance, that rapid initial advancement is neither sustained nor permanent, and mere performance in a skill is little guide to its use to the individual. While communication embraces a complex of skills, achievement in a number of these skills in isolation does not add up to competence in communication as a whole. Practice in making the one-to-one correspondence between the printed and the spoken word, for instance, does not necessarily lead to understanding of what is read. The ideas behind the words must be mentally organised before meaning becomes available to the reader, and preoccupation with the visible and audible part of the process can prevent this from taking place.

While we do not leave the learning of communication skills to chance, we hasten the child through the processes involved to the detriment of individual and social competence in making use of these skills.

Of all types of communication, language, or human speech in both written and spoken form, is the most explicit. As a result it holds a supremely eminent place in education, and much time and energy is devoted to developing and practising verbal communication skills. What we must not forget is that in the child's early learning, non-verbal communication precedes verbal communication. Throughout his early years, when verbal skills are emerging, the child continues to rely heavily on gesture, mime, movement and intonation to convey and obtain meaning. His communication strengths are in these areas and this is where he has confidence. As adults we are often unaware of the contribution of non-verbal skills in communication, yet few of us depend entirely on words if we want to get at the actual message. Sometimes words spoken contradict the glance or gesture which accompanies them, and all of us have suffered from the inadequacy of the printed word in conveying meaning precisely.

The child has an aptitude for 'seeing through' what is said to him, because he depends on non-verbal signals for his clues, and many adults frankly acknowledge the fact that it is difficult to deceive a child. Perhaps, as adults, we would make fewer mistakes in our relations with others if we paid more attention to non-verbal signals. As it is, we leave that to the psychologist who is then thought to be more able than his colleagues to understand human nature. In this respect we have much to learn from children, and we must never despise, or underestimate, the value of those many modes of communication which come easily to the child.

Chapter 7

Grasping mathematical ideas

Mathematical ideas available to the child fall broadly into three categories: ideas about measurement, about shape, and about numbers. These three categories overlap considerably and in planning experience we need to remember this. We use numbers, for example, in defining measurements, and we use the concept of length when dealing with shapes. It is also helpful to remember that at each stage in cognitive development there is close correspondence between different ideas. When a child, for instance, is able to estimate with some degree of accuracy the length of straight or curved lines, he should be able, given suitable experience, to estimate the weight of an object that he can hold in his hand.

Ideas about measurement include time, weight, length, capacity, area and money. The developmental pattern of any one of these (for example, weight) will serve as a guide to the way in which a child can be led from stage to stage towards understanding an abstract mathematical concept.

Like other mathematical notions, the concept of weight originates in miscellaneous experiences of daily life, and develops through concrete experiences of increasing complexity towards an abstract idea which can be applied in many ways. From his play experiences the child learns that some objects have more effect on his muscles than others. An object which can only be moved with effort is 'heavy', one which can be moved easily is 'light'. The child does not know at this stage that these terms are relative, and if a bucket of sand feels 'heavy' to him then, to his way of thinking, it feels heavy to anyone else. Sand becomes known to him as 'heavy', and he finds difficulty in entertaining the idea that a few grains of sand could be 'light'.

The child entering school needs first to improve and refine his knowledge of such terms. In one classroom a selection of objects was set out on a table and the children were encouraged to handle and discuss them and to say whether they were heavy or light. With some objects opinion was divided, and a 'middling' group of objects was assembled. The teacher introduced the use of the term 'lighter than' and 'heavier than', and eventually 'not so light as', etc. One child selected a ball of wool, a piece of chalk and a wooden cube. After balancing each from hand to hand she set them in a row with the chalk in the middle. Then she pointed to the chalk. 'That's heavy *and* light', she decided. 'If I put it in the middle it's heavier than the wool and lighter than the cube.'

The effect of differences in weight, even minor differences, is clearly illustrated by a see-saw, and the idea of balance is associated with differences and with finding the point at which they disappear. Large balance pans and a box full of assorted objects such as beads, washers, marbles, dog biscuits, buttons, etc., enable the child to compare one object with another, or to compare a single object with a number of others. A progression on this is to decide an order by weight of a number of objects, and this experience offers a hint about the relationships, or lack of them, between size and weight.

At some point in experimentation the child discovers satisfaction in making things balance. He may have noticed this interesting phenomenon while watching his mother preparing ingredients when baking, or buying meat for Sunday lunch. In his own experiments the child may at first use his hand to make the trick work, but later he learns how to balance the pans so that they remain still. The result gives him great satisfaction and pleasure, and he may prolong this stage for its aesthetic value.

Surprise parcels may now be used to explore the idea that weight and size are not related unless the parcels contain the same kind of material. All one-pound bags of sugar, for instance, are similar in size, but a pound of lead shot would make a much smaller parcel. Some children find this idea difficult to grasp and even a sensible boy of six-and-a-half may insist that the big parcel is heavier in spite of proof to the contrary. Experience and cognitive growth combine to bring the idea to fruition, and a few weeks later the same child may ridicule similar ignorance on the part of his companions.

During the next stage regular units can be used as a means of comparing amounts of matter. Beads, grains of rice, glass marbles, etc., are suitable basic units against which other objects can be balanced. The same principle is employed to compare objects, and a child may record that 'the little doll balanced six marbles and the big doll balanced twelve marbles'. The more able child may grasp the idea that 'the big doll is double (twice as heavy as) the little doll', or 'the little doll is half the weight of the big doll'.

Activities such as cooking provide opportunities for using the idea of comparison, e.g. the weight of one egg in fat and sugar, together with the same quantity of flour as fat and sugar combined, is a measure of the ingredients for one kind of cake mixture. Cooking also introduces and illustrates the need for accuracy in weighing. Too much or too little shortening in pastry mix renders the product inedible. The balance between ingredients must be maintained, and we need stable units with which to compare the respective amounts used. This idea is reinforced for the child when he buys sweets. There are still a few items that can be purchased by weight, and each child buying the same small sum's worth of toffees must receive the same amount for his money.

When ideas of comparison are well established, standardised units may be introduced. A large number of single small units, such as ounces, can replace the marbles or beads, and objects can be compared according to the number of ounces they balance. When the pound, half-pound and quarter-pound weights are introduced the child can 'discover' and check their value by balancing each against the one ounce weights. Otherwise 'a half', or 'a quarter' may mean to the child the name of a weight rather than that it is equivalent to a fixed number of ounce weights. Some children need much experience before they comprehend the relationship between the various units or understand why we use a large unit which is divisible into smaller units.

Experience enables the child to estimate the weight of objects which he can handle and he will enjoy the game of checking his guess and recording errors. Balance pans are not the only means of checking weight and the child can be introduced to a wide range of instruments used in weighing, from kitchen scales and the spring balance to personal weighing machines and a weigh bridge. Simple weighing devices can be made by the child as an aid to understanding the principles involved. Exploring the uses of these instruments adds much to the child's developing ideas.

When these foundational ideas are well established, the child is ready for shopping experiences in which real materials are used. A simulated supermarket with dummy packets and plastic money scarcely leads to accurate concepts, the child learns more from a real shopping experience once a week than he would from daily play with dummy packets. In one school the children make sweets and sell them by weight each Friday afternoon, and when parents visit they make cakes and biscuits and sell them with cups of tea. Everyday events such as these offer good weighing and other mathematical experiences. There is always more to be learned from realistic situations and this is particularly true where mathematics is concerned.

The child knows through the messages he receives from his muscles that weight is 'pulling down', and a few children of seven or eight may begin to understand gravitational pull, although this is a highly abstract idea which will not fully mature until a much later stage. Space travel films introduce the child to the effects of weightlessness, or the absence of gravitational pull, but full comprehension of this idea must wait until the child is capable of handling the abstract.

The development of other mathematical ideas follows a similar pattern. Understanding of shape, for example, does not come from observing and naming the square, the circle and the triangle. The ability to recognise and name these figures contributes little to the child's concept of shape, for they are two-dimensional formal figures, and foundational ideas about shape develop through handling three-dimensional, solid, regular and irregular objects such as the child uses in everyday life. Right from birth the shape of things plays an important part in the child's life and through manipulating such objects as a mug or a bottle, a ball or a rattle, his foot or a shoe, the significance of shape is brought home to the child.

In one classroom a study of shape was developed along the following lines. The teacher assembled a display of interesting shapes which included a wooden rattle, an African drum, a Chinese abacus, a tricorn shell, a dried bean pod, spoons made of wood, bone and metal, a mug and a lump of alabaster. Some of these shapes were already thoroughly familiar, others were not. Each object was discussed with references to its purpose and aesthetic qualities. Where many of the objects were concerned the children supplied the information, with others the teacher first encouraged speculation (for example about the use of the abacus) and then added facts herself.

Next day the children were asked to sort out the objects, deciding their own criteria. This they did according to use, colour, size, preference, etc. Eventually the objects were divided into two groups, one of 'real' things, the other of 'things made by people', and a fundamental principle had been grasped.

Attention was then focused on spoons and the children made a collection of spoons fashioned from different materials. Discussion led to the conclusions that they were all used for a similar purpose, that they were 'like one another', but that 'some were thick and some were thin and some were middling'. The material from which they were made obviously influenced the design, and the idea that material as well as purpose determines shape began to emerge.

The children then 'made shapes' in clay, and looked at the surfaces and edges of their shapes. Some were curved and some were flat, some had edges and corners, others were curved without edges, etc. At a later stage the children worked in pairs. They made collections of objects and thought of ways in which they could set them out in a row. To begin with, they set them out in any order. Then they began to make rules and set out the objects in order of size, height, width, etc.

Next they threaded straws to make polygonal shapes. They were then able to concentrate on edges and corners. Only when they were thoroughly familiar with the way in which boundaries determined shapes were they introduced to two-dimensional, regular shapes, which they identified as surfaces of a particular kind. They were then ready to find similar shapes in their environment and to assemble objects which had, for example, square surfaces. The children were later provided with sets of squares and triangles and were invited to make patterns and to cover surfaces by fitting the shapes together.

This study was spread over a period of several weeks and not all of the children reached the final stage. Many spent a considerable time over the clay shapes and some progressed no further, but remained thoroughly involved in making shapes with clay. The way they handled the material, however, indicated their intensified interest in the shapes which they created. Even the less able children became shape-conscious.

In recent years, intensified interest in mathematics and in the child's mathematical understanding has led to improvement in the way number experiences are structured. Well-organised work in sorting, classification and ordering and numbering can be found in an increasing number of classrooms. Unfortunately provision for mathematical experience frequently focuses on numbering and counting, when similar attention needs to be paid to every aspect of mathematical experience if the child's mathematical education is to be complete.

To take just one further example, let us look at the growth of ideas about time—one of the most abstract and therefore most difficult ideas for a child to grasp. Once speech is established as part of the child's daily life, we can look for evidence of his growing ideas in the comments he makes. 'At night' or 'when it is day again' are comments which indicate an attempt on the part of the child to pinpoint an event. 'Now' is one of the first time words a child understands, and 'tomorrow' may mean 'not for a long time'. 'Yesterday' is even more difficult and one hears five-year-olds explaining it as 'not today, that other day'. Looking towards what is to come, he may get as far as 'not the next day but that other day', meaning the day after tomorrow. From his point of view an event occurring two or three days ahead may seem as remote as this time next year. Even his notion of time already experienced is understood in terms of what it meant to him. 'That day when I fell down and cut my knee' may be his way of describing 'last Friday'.

The incidence of his sixth birthday reminds the child that he 'had a birthday before', and he hopefully expects to have 'another next time'. Some children fail to grasp the fact that a birthday occurs on the same date each year. One seven-year-old was firmly convinced that 'My birthday was in April when I was six, but I'm having it in May this year'. The six-year-old recognises the days of the week and may be able to name them, and experience of school will help him to give certain days a sense of identity. 'When it's Friday it'll be Saturday and Sunday after and we're going camping.' He is now beginning to understand the sequence factor in time. Sequence and rhythm have much in common, and the child's inborn sense of rhythm is a great pleasure to him from birth, and this can be used by the adult in helping him to clarify his ideas of sequence.

Games such as 'Pat-a-cake', 'This Little Pig', etc., popular in the child's pre-school years, are built round his love of rhythm and introduce the idea of one thing following another. The five-year-old enjoys repetitional stories ('and the next day', or 'and then', or the accumulative story such as 'Henny Penny', or 'The Tale of the Turnip') in which a sequence of ideas is gradually constructed. Counting games such as 'One potato, two potatoes, etc.' include rhythmic sequence. The child's attention can be drawn to the sequence of events in the day. 'First it's breakfast time, then we come to school, then it's dinner time, etc.' 'What comes before dinner? . . . after tea? etc.' Discussion, in terms of before and after, of the child's experiences during a week will follow. By the time he is six the child begins to grasp the sequence of events in a year. Much of this work is incidental, but the teacher who is aware of the child's developing ideas can use many incidents and routines as a means of increasing his grasp of the order of events.

The idea of duration also develops from personal experience of 'how long things last'. A long time may mean two minutes when a hungry child is waiting for lunch, or holding his breath, or keeping still, whereas the same child is totally unaware of the passage of time during play. Experiments with a food-timer, egg-timer, or an alarm clock will expand the child's ideas, but a sound notion of time passing is unlikely to develop during the early school years. Indeed, few adults have a fully developed sense of duration.

Although in a closely synchronised society learning to read the clock face is an important skill, it does not in itself add much to the child's concept of time. Recognising special times on the clock face can be associated with the idea of sequence and later of duration, and many children of seven are able to tell the time. A large clock which forms part of the life of the classroom is the most effective aid. Cardboard clock faces, or clock faces stamped on paper, may provide exercises in memorising the position of the hands and the spaces between them, but children learn these things far more effectively from a real clock, even if it is broken and discarded, so long as the hands will still rotate.

Most children of six know the names of the days in the week, but not all of them can put them in order. In the majority of class-rooms, weather records, news sheets, job schedules and the like are used to help the child to establish ideas about the calendar, and this aspect of time is usually well covered. Birthdays also play a prominent part in the social life of the classroom, and birth dates can be marked up on the calendar. In one classroom the children use a calendar solely for this purpose, and birthdays are marked through the calendar at the beginning of the year.

The seven-year-old has many time experiences which need clarifying and drawing together. One group of children, when asked 'What is a day?', gave the following replies. 'It's a day now and there are other days. There are seven days and they all have different names.' 'A day is when you buy a ticket and come back to go to bed.' 'When it's light.' 'You get up and you go to bed and in between it's a day.'

They then discussed what a year was and the seasons were mentioned. 'It's all because of the sun,' one child explained. 'It gets hot and then we have summer.' The teacher used this opportunity to draw the attention of the children to the behaviour of the sun during the year, and later, with her help, the children constructed a model which illustrated the journey of the earth round the sun and the consequences of this.

The same group of children were asked to draw the shape of the moon at bedtime (seven o'clock) each night during two or three weeks of clear January weather. The idea of the lunar month is difficult to grasp, but at the end of their observations these children could answer the questions, 'What is the shape of the new moon?', 'At what time in the night and where would you expect to see it?' and 'What is the shape of the moon when it is waning?' There are a great many experienced teachers who would give incorrect answers to these questions!

The child who can tell the time, or whose interest in the clock has been thoroughly aroused, will be interested in primitive timing devices, and constructing sand, candle or water clocks, or a sundial, will add richly to his ideas of duration and precision. There is scarcely any place in the infant school for arithmetic employing hours, days, months, etc., but simple timetables which are part of the organisation of daily activities, or have a role in dramatic play, are within the comprehension of children of seven and eight.

Chapter 12 includes extracts from a teacher's recorded observation of the way in which one boy's ideas of time developed over a period of fifteen months. Such records are a much more accurate guide to the quality of the child's ideas than his performance in working out clock sums.

Chapter 8

Learning to socialise

Experience plays a major role in every aspect of a child's development. In social development experience of other people is the only means of helping a child to become a social being, and the adult who knows what to expect of a child in the way of interpersonal reaction can plan suitable challenges for him at each stage in his social growth.

Much happens in the pre-school years, of course, and this often affects what the teacher can do. The kind of relationship which the child makes with his parents and with adults outside the home, the opportunity he has to play with another child, to observe and imitate other people, together with his characteristic attitude to the world and the people he meets in it, provide a background against which teacher and child must work.

Social experience under the guidance of a trained teacher is one of the major advantages of nursery and infant schools. With a teacher in control, the vast opportunities for contact with people outside the home become available to the child at a stage in his development when he most needs them. Many parents recognise this unique role of the teacher, and the child growing up in even a privileged home is often brought to the nursery school by a parent who acknowledges its function in providing experience which the home cannot provide.

Many children in the nursery school and a few in the infant school need to engage in solitary play, even though they have adequate contact with other children. They may progress rather slowly through the stages of learning to play with one other child and learning how to make good contact with adults, before they are ready to belong to a group and discover their own particular role in a group.

Most five-year-olds, however, are ready to make friendly approaches to other children and to play together in small groups. Relationships at this stage are experimental and group play remains very fluid. Groups split up and re-form. Speech is often limited and conflict is dealt with in a physical way. While a certain amount of squabbling, even fighting, is part of the socialising process, of discovering the give as well as the take of group membership, the watchful teacher makes sure that no child is bossed about, or made miserable by another child. As far as possible the teacher guarantees pleasurable social contact as a means of establishing good social attitudes during these foundational stages. At this stage the teacher does not insist on children working together consistently in groups, unless she is there to hold the group together.

Between five and six years old, the child can be helped to become more aware of other people and of his own attitudes towards others. When a squabble arises, the adult is given the opportunity to help each of the parties concerned to see the situation from differing points of view. Putting himself in the shoes of another child is a difficult task for the six-year-old and he may not succeed at the first attempt. But the argument of the adult has some force behind it to which he may at first give grudging recognition, before he begins to comprehend the sense of it.

Dave, aged six, constructed a train from boxes, and the dolls from the house corner were installed as passengers. Sue, aged four, seeing her favourite dolly sitting in one of the boxes, trotted across the room and claimed it. Dave turned, indignant; 'She can't do that,' he shouted in the direction of his vigilant teacher. But for her he would surely have confirmed his rights in a more obvious way. 'I got the dolls first and she's got to wait till I've finished playing with them.'

Dave's teacher explained. 'Sue's only four and you're six, Dave. She doesn't know much about making things fair yet. She has to learn like you did. Why not ask Sue if dolly would like a ride?' Dave stared at Sue for a moment. She cradled her dolly, blissfully unaware of the storm. Then his attitude changed. 'I've made a train to take all the dollies,' he said to Sue. 'You can help me to pull if you like.' Encouraged by his friendly approach, Sue beamed. 'You can go on the train,' she said to the dolly. 'I'm going to be the engine with Dave.'

Awareness of other people helps the child to become aware of the importance of the opinion of others and of the need to gain approval. The rules of companionship are established by his companions and are influenced by the leadership of the adult. In the classroom the teacher enables companionship to bring reward to all who participate. She keeps a firm control over the more dominant characters in her class and encourages the timid and apprehensive child to receive as well as give. In this way companionship becomes a desirable goal for every child, and the approval of those who can offer it is a very persuasive discipline.

What happened between six-year-old Paul and his companions illustrates the way in which factors such as these encourage the child to modify his own behaviour. Large junk play on the playground was the source of much vigorous and imaginative play for a group of six-year-old boys. Irrespective of weather conditions, they commandeered 'the boxes' whenever their teacher allowed them to go outside. Paul was an intelligent and highly imaginative child. At first he didn't join in the junk play and ideas were well under way when he finally decided to do so.

Within minutes, Paul had planned a game which he called 'Pirates', in which the junk was piled in different parts of the playground and the journey from pile to pile was to be made without touching the ground. At first the other boys accepted Paul's lead because his ideas attracted them. Paul began to improve on his original idea and new rules were added to the game. The penalty for breaking the rules was exclusion from the game, and Paul's imaginative ideas led him towards sole domination of the junk. 'I'm Pirate King,' he announced triumphantly. 'Now all this lot belongs to me and you must do what I tell you if you want to come on my land.'

To begin with, the other boys gave way to Paul. Then one by one they abandoned the game and re-grouped to make other plans. Left alone in his territory, Paul's power dwindled. There wasn't much fun in having complete control of the junk if others weren't there to make the game interesting. A week later the junk play was again in full swing. Paul was still a lively member of the group, but he had learned how far he was allowed to go and he was prepared to submit himself to the discipline of the group in order to belong to it.

The six- and seven-year-old child is socially confident enough to submit himself to the rules of a more cohesive group, and gang play begins to emerge. This stage needs careful handling. The gang has the accumulated energy of all its members, and this is energy which the adult may use, but not ignore or suppress.

In schools where the children are vertically grouped and there is no concentration of any one age group in a class, the gang has less opportunity to form. From the teacher's point of view this is often noticed with considerable relief. From the child's point of view gang play marks a stage in social development, and although the gang may lack cohesion in school, in neighbourhoods where parents allow their children to play freely beyond the confines of the home itself gangs of seven-year-olds readily form. Sometimes these emergent gangs are absorbed by groups of older children who may have been commissioned by parents to 'keep an eye on young Jimmy'.

There are still many schools in which the seven-year-olds are grouped together and we can see from the following example how important the teacher's influence is in setting the mood for this stage in group behaviour.

The seven-year-old gang is basically a play group, intent on finding fun and having a good time, and almost inevitably this leads to finding fun in making mischief. The gang formed among children in Miss Turner's class consisted solely of boys whose main interest centred on vigorous physical activity and who took possession of play apparatus such as wagons and climbing frames the minute they left her classroom.

Miss Turner realised that she must find an outlet for this collective energy before this gang began to dominate the rest of the school, herself included. The school was situated near a group of garden allotments. Miss Turner persuaded the local education authority to rent one of the allotments on the understanding that her gardeners would work there only under her supervision.

'I need some very strong boys,' she explained to the class. 'We have a garden and we can grow things to eat in it. If we work hard we shall have some nice peas and beans and new potatoes.'

The idea caught on. She provided each member of the gang with a full-size spade, fork or rake, and each lunchtime was devoted to hard labour. Healthy expenditure of energy rendered the young men amenable for the rest of the day. Miss Turner expected a few problems and she experienced one or two uncomfortable moments, but most of the boys enjoyed the challenge enormously and earned themselves a major share in the produce, which they took home to their approving parents.

Sex differences also begin to affect relationships in late infancy, and it is usually girls who initiate behaviour which emphasises the difference between boys and girls. The seven-year-old sweetheart game is often started by a girl, while juvenile prowess in response to this has a marked effect on the behaviour of boys. Society has helped to mould the idea of what is acceptable behaviour in boys and in girls, and as their interests begin to diverge they find pleasure in belonging to groups of their own sex. Many boys become distinctly aggressive and sometimes this aggression is turned on the opposite sex, with the result that girls refuse to associate on friendly terms with boys and some may fight back. Curiosity about sex differences sometimes draws the sexes together, and hospital or house play may become secretive.

The teacher who takes note of these divergent tendencies does not attempt to group antagonistic boys and girls together. At times it is wiser to let the aggressors work things out between themselves, making sure that they take it out of one another and not out of more passive members of the group. The present-day trend towards interest-based work has helped in many classrooms to minimise sex antagonism, and younger children may show little tendency in this direction if their work is self-fulfilling.

The emergence of leadership is another interesting development among the sixes and sevens. From the moment two children play together one child tends to take the lead, and with younger children girls tend to take the leadership role. Where the children have considerable freedom in school, the leader tends to be the child with superior physical and social attributes. In schools where the adult offers firm direction, the intellectually able child is often chosen to lead. As the gang stage is reached, leadership becomes more pronounced, and the teacher who is aware of the natural leaders in her class has an excellent opportunity to gain their co-operation. To work unwittingly against them can be disastrous.

The teacher's aim in handling social tendencies is to promote harmony in the group, and the work of the class is greatly enhanced by the establishment of a harmonious social atmosphere in the classroom. Activities such as house play and other forms of spontaneous drama offer excellent social experience, and a well designed and maintained house corner and dressing-up box are essential classroom equipment.

Although children need freedom from adult domination in dramatic play, the teacher has an important function in the house corner. By paying attention to what happens there, encouraging children to keep it clean and tidy, or to make new curtains, clothes, pictures and other equipment for it, she can help to make this a corner which children respect. (More is said about this in Chapter 5 on developmental drama.) Children learn to co-operate with one another by working co-operatively together, not by being taught 'good manners' and 'obedience,' and good dramatic play makes for good social atmosphere in the classroom.

A major social development during these years is in the growth of the child's attitudes towards adults. Many children enter school with little close experience of adults other than those in the family which is responsible for rearing them and to whom they are bound by relationship ties. Making a good relationship with adults to whom they are not emotionally linked is a new and sometimes difficult experience. Acceptance by the teacher establishes the child's confidence in making good contact with an adult outside the home. Although the teacher has responsibility for him, she is not emotionally bound up in his personal life and she provides a bridging experience between relatives and strangers.

In the school community there are a number of adults such as domestic assistants, maintenance men, the caretaker and other members of staff, together with adults who visit the school such as advisers, social workers, college lecturers, publishers and inspectors. All of these can be used by the teacher in helping the child to learn how to approach strangers, how to help visitors, how to learn from helpful adults, and how to respect the rights of adults in the home and outside it. In determining his future role as a responsible citizen, respect freely shown by the child in approaching others is far more effective than authority imposed on him. Visitors to a school quickly sense the influence of the teacher in developing social attitudes from the way in which they are received by the children. There is a world of difference between being approached helpfully but respectfully by a friendly six-year-old, and facing a 'Good morning' chorus from a class which stands to attention the moment a visitor is introduced.

One of the most desirable social qualities is co-operation, and it is during the first years in school that this may be developed. Children do not become helpful by being told it is a good thing, but the adult can plan experiences in which they learn to appreciate its benefits.

During their first months in school most children remain basically egocentric. This is perfectly normal, and persuading, forcing, or even expecting a child to be helpful may be unrealistic. He needs first to be at the receiving end of the benefits because someone offers him help. The teacher helps a cold-fingered child with his buttons. An older or more able child offers help, or is asked to help, a less able colleague. The child responds with a feeling of gratitude, comfort, or pleasure, and this experience is one which he will later wish to give to others.

The true spirit of helping is not expressed in an act performed in order to secure approval, or to placate one who has power to satisfy needs. Helping both rewards the helper by enlarging his idea of himself, and eases the burden of the one helped. It can also bring mutual benefit when a task is accomplished together which neither could perform singly.

The child who lacks confidence feels unable to help since, in his own eyes, he is of no account and has little to offer. The teacher may need to help such a child to make a small beginning by finding some way in which he can be of assistance to her. 'I can't read this story without my glasses. Will you fetch them from my desk for me please, James?' James does this successfully and receives the reward not only of his teacher's smile, but of the gratitude of children who are waiting for the story. James feels temporarily ten feet tall.

The demand on James is increased when he is asked to help a colleague. 'Robert can't carry the bricks by himself. Will you give him a hand, James?' This time James has the rewarding experience of sharing another's load, albeit briefly, and he glimpses what it means to be needed and to be of use. Later James is required to make a more sustained effort and to offer valuable service to the group. 'Every time we clear away we must check the scissors to make sure none are lost. Can you do that, James?'

In this way James is led from helping the adult he finds easy to please, through helping another child, to offering help for the benefit of the community. He may still have to learn the advantages of working with others, for instance, in making a model. One day he will see for himself where he could be of use and proffer spontaneous assistance. 'Can I help Dave to paint his box, so's it won't take him so long?'—James will now begin to find genuine pleasure in giving without expecting a return, and the basic rules of co-operation will have been learned.

Thousands of teachers in charge of young children are so sensitive to their social problems that help of this kind is given generously and often unwittingly. Others would willingly help but are not always aware of how to set about it, or tend to expect too much of a child, or expect him to mature too quickly. Awareness of the child's slowly maturing progress towards social confidence and adjustment enables any teacher to help more effectively.

We should never assume that merely by bringing children together we help them to socialise. Without the planned assistance of the teacher, some children make little headway toward social maturity. It is in the early years of schooling that ideas about a well-structured community and the attitudes and contribution of the individual in helping to make that community successful begin to emerge and take shape as the foundation on which the whole pattern of society is structured.

Chapter 9

The maturing emotions

At any age emotions have a powerful influence on every aspect of a person's life. In the early years the child's emotional life is in supreme command, and what he feels constitutes the child's awareness of himself. Although the child is born able to respond emotionally, learning plays an important part in developing the emotions, and the environment in which the child is reared determines the way in which his emotions mature. The pattern of development leading towards maturity begins in the baby's general feelings of either pleasure and comfort, or dissatisfaction and discomfort, and works towards the identification of specific emotions such as joy, excitement and love, or fear, anger, anxiety and hate. Behavioural patterns learned in the early years of life become habitual and act as driving forces to help or hinder adjustment. Behavioural habits influence the individual's view of people and events, and determine his characteristic reactions to his environment. The adults on whom the child depends provide basic emotional experiences in which his feelings mature.

Whatever emotional maturity may mean, it is usually regarded as a desirable goal, and there is a strong tendency on the part of many adults to expect mature behaviour before the child has achieved it. Adequate experience is essential to emotional education and the child must have time to learn about his emotions. He needs to be four, five or six long enough to learn what it means to be that age, and we do not help the child by encouraging him to behave like a ten-year-old while he is still five. On the other hand, we must not hold him back, and treating him like a three-year-old when he is emotionally five also leads to poor adjustment.

We must protect the child against misguided ambitions on the part of some educators and many parents to produce children who have outstripped their years. Why do we devote so much energy and time to 'early achievement', 'boosting the child's I.Q.', and 'hastening maturation'? Why is the parent so proud of the child who is 'advanced for his age'? Why do we conspire against childhood by setting our sights on producing instant adults and consequently by-passing the patient growth of the foundational years? We may be able to hustle the child through his formative years and even produce precocious results, but we should think seriously before we attempt this, as we can never restore to the child the years we have stolen.

To let a child be his age is not an easy task for the adult. Children and adults view the world in very different ways, with the result that misunderstanding creates a serious barrier between the two, and frequently, unintentionally, much damage is done.

The four- or five-year-old is basically egocentric, and although he is aware of himself and of other selves as separate entities, he still believes that the world centres on him. Nicholas, nearing the age of five, was watching television when a news film showed Asian evacuees receiving parcels of clothing. He leaned forward. 'Have they got my pullover yet?' he asked, fully expecting to see it worn by a small Indian boy. On another occasion, when told by his aunt that she had been to a meeting to 'talk about the under-fives', he enquired eagerly, 'I'm under five. What did you say about me?'

A teacher may feel off colour and ask her five-year-olds to play more quietly because she has a headache. Naturally she feels resentful when the children to whom she devotes her energies take little notice, or even increase their demands. What she may not realise is that the five-year-old either feels annoyed when the attention he seeks is withdrawn, or rejected because his teacher is putting her needs before his own.

One student teacher had considerable success in telling stories to a five-year-old group. She managed to catch and hold their attention and felt well rewarded for the effort she put into preparing her story. A few days later she was to take the period again and spent a whole evening preparing her new story. From the moment she embarked on her story she realised that it was not to their liking. They began to fidget and to talk to one another. Five minutes later the group she had expected to hold spellbound were squirming around in a noisy huddle. 'When I'd been to so much trouble,' she complained later, 'the least they could do would be to sit still and listen.' What she learned from this experience was that small children have no notion of the idea that they should appreciate effort expended on their behalf.

Children reason, but not in the same way as adults, and emotional reaction often dominates the way they behave. Their reasons are predominantly emotionally based, and logical or verbal reasoning play a subordinate part in their decisions. Wendy was shown a row of doll's beds graded in size and was asked to put a graded set of dolls to bed. She carefully placed the smallest doll in the biggest bed. 'Because she's so little,' she explained tenderly. The doll needed compensating and this was a perfectly valid reason for Wendy's decision.

David was shown a picture of a row of houses. He was given the numerals 1 to 5 and asked to put them on the right doors. He looked carefully at each numeral and then selected 4 and put it on the first door. 'I live at number 4,' he explained, 'so it's the best.' He liked the number which represented his home and therefore he gave it priority, and he did so in spite of the fact that he knew his numerals and could count.

The young child has little idea of time, and the present and how he feels are all that matters to him. To be told that he will see mother again at dinner time when he is parted from her for the first time in his life does not take away the dreadful feeling of being deserted by her. When a five-year-old is hungry we should not sit him down at the table and keep him waiting. His stomach is screaming out in anguish and to wait for food is sheer agony. The five- and six-year-old child is not persuaded to work hard at his reading by being assured that he will enjoy it when he is seven. He needs reward for his efforts immediately, and this is the only form of motivation to which he responds, for the emotional experience of the moment is all that he understands.

The five-year-old comprehends an incident by the way in which it affects him. If Granny dies, that means she won't be in her bungalow with the chocolate cake she's made for his tea, and he grieves for himself rather than for her. Mother may need to enter hospital and she tells her little girl, 'I shan't be away long, darling. I have a bad pain and the hospital will make it better.' In spite of the fact that her father tries to hide his preoccupation and anxiety, and takes his little daughter to visit her mother daily, the child feels rejected and resentful. Mother doesn't love her any more, otherwise she would be there to tuck her in at bedtime. She may fret, or become unruly and add to her father's problems at the worst possible time.

Another important quality of the child's early emotional life is the intensity of feelings experienced for the first time. As adults we have learned to understand and, to a certain extent, control our emotions, and we have enough experience of them to know what to expect. Even so, we are sometimes caught unawares, or have an unfamiliar emotional experience which makes us feel 'beside ourselves' or 'not ourselves'. 'I don't know what came over me,' we say, or 'I don't know what made me behave like that.' We acknowledge and fear the power of love, hate, jealousy and fear in ourselves. We should remember that, for the six- or seven-year-old, feelings are even more powerful.

Curiosity is particularly strong in early childhood and it may motivate far more powerfully than love, hate, or even jealousy. In adult life we rarely experience the drive of curiosity intense enough to make us poke the new baby to find out whether he's a 'proper person,' or what, in fact, he is like. 'The trouble is,' one thoughtful seven-year-old pondered, 'I know some things live and some things don't, and that those that live can feel, but I don't know which things feel like me.' Adults must try to understand feelings in the child which they themselves have forgotten.

The child's early emotional life falls broadly into four stages. In his pre-school days, the feelings which bind him and his mother together are completely fused. He learns from her how to love and be loved, and it is she who sets the pattern for future intimate relationships. In the modern home the child tends to have comparatively little contact with his father, who is usually regarded as the provider and sometimes the disciplinarian. Many children of both sexes turn readily to any male figure they may find on entering nursery or infant school. This seems to indicate a deep-seated need for more physical and intellectual contact with the father figure, and there is a case for employing male teachers for the under sevens. As it is, early relationship experiences are based mainly on mother contact and the child who has no interest in other people is the child who has not experienced warmth and love in his mother's protecting arms. Such a child is emotionally handicapped and may never know the personal fulfilment of a completely satisfactory relationship.

Important as this relationship is, the child needs to become to some extent emotionally independent of his mother before he can learn to accept and respond to another adult, or even another child, and the child who remains bound by his mother's love may be equally handicapped when it comes to making a satisfactory relationship. Some five-year-olds are still over-dependent on entering school, and the teacher may have her work cut out in helping both mother and child to allow one another a measure of freedom. This is a familiar problem and it may be of interest to see how one teacher tried to solve it.

Vanessa was an only child and when mother brought her to school soon after her fifth birthday she looked more like a well-dressed doll than a child. 'I don't think she's going to settle,' mother said tearfully, 'and the house will be empty without her.' She turned to the child. 'Are you going to like it here, my darling? Mother won't leave you till you feel happy.' Vanessa screwed up her face and clutched her mother's coat. 'No!' She began to stamp. 'Nasty school! I want to go home with you.'

The teacher watched patiently for a moment. 'There!' Mother was triumphant. 'She never has gone to strangers.' The teacher remained unimpressed. 'I can see that,' she said. 'Well it's a pity, but she's not really ready to make the break, is she? I think you'd better take her home and get her used to being away from you, before you try to leave her here.'

The mother was shaken. She'd expected a scene in which her daughter's devotion to her mother would be made clear to this other woman. It had never entered her head that she might not be allowed to leave Vanessa. Her attitude changed.

'There, there, Vanessa,' she coaxed. 'Be a good girl. The teacher will look after you, and you're big enough now to stay by yourself.' Vanessa wasn't prepared to play this new game and her sobs increased.

'I'm sorry,' the teacher said, holding her ground. 'I'm sure that when you get Vanessa used to the idea of being left with me, she will be happy here. As it is, she's upsetting the others. So will you please take her home now, and bring her back next week.'

She was determined to make the mother face up to her responsibility, and she remained gentle but firm. 'If Vanessa is ready to be left next week,' she said, 'we'll try her for an hour or two each day at first, and gradually build up to the full day.' It was a month before Vanessa felt free to enjoy school and her mother began to loosen the fetters.

Between the ages of five and six most children begin to enjoy sharing experiences with others, and through doing this they learn to develop a sense of companionship. These moods, however, are often short-lived. Children who appear to play happily together for perhaps twenty minutes may suddenly change their companions, or revert to isolated, or parallel play. In the course of one morning, Julian moved from one play interest to another seven times. Each change of activity brought him into contact with fresh companions and within a few minutes he had settled with one of them, but for only a very short time. Finally he broke right away from the rest of the class and went into the hall where musical instruments were arranged in one corner. He spent the rest of the morning experimenting with the various sounds. Cilla, on the other hand, attached herself to an older girl as soon as she entered the classroom. The older girl took the lead and Cilla happily agreed to whatever the older girl suggested. Although the two stayed together through the morning, the companionship was unequal and destined to last only as long as the older girl found it satisfying.

Many children are seven before they become capable of sharing at a level which makes real friendship possible. The child at this stage has learned a lot about himself and is well advanced in understanding his own feelings. He can, at least for brief periods, put himself in his companion's shoes. He wants his companion to enjoy the game too. His happiness is increased by helping his companion to be happy, and this makes friendship possible.

From now on, friendships grow in strength and duration. The most satisfactory friendships are those between equals, and most children tend to make friends with others who have similar interests and characteristics. This kind of friendship enables a child to make rapid strides in his emotional development. A friendship which is rewarding is worth working for, and in a healthy friendship each child will learn to be generous, even-tempered, honest, sporting and ready to put the needs of another before his own. If the friendship is ill-balanced it may become one in which one child dominates and the other becomes submissive, and such a friendship is less valuable in fostering emotional growth. In a balanced friendship, each partner feels thoroughly at home and able to communicate, bound to the other and yet free to develop as an individual. The vigilant teacher can do much to encourage those friendships which provide experience leading to mature relationships. She may likewise discourage relationships which stunt emotional growth, although children need to experiment with many types of relationship in order to understand what true friendship is about.

The young child always strives towards personal independence and responsibility. The teacher has a unique opportunity to further this aim. She deals with each child as one of a group and is much more able than his parents to view him objectively. She sees him as he is in comparison with other children. He is neither of her, nor does he belong to her, and the challenging nature of her relationship with him helps him to get to know himself as an individual apart from his family. She encourages him to stand on his own two feet and think for himself. Step by step she shows him the satisfaction of making decisions and then taking the responsibility for the outcome of his choices.

Tony and some of his friends were making a model chalet in connection with an interest in Switzerland which had developed as a result of a recent holiday visit. A teacher in another part of the school was showing a film on Switzerland and he sent a message to say that there were seats for one or two more.

Tony's first reaction was to go and see the film, but the other boys in the group wanted to carry on with the model. So far the group had worked under Tony's leadership and he was loath to relinquish his position. He turned to his teacher. 'I want to see the film,' he said. 'But this lot'll do it all wrong if I go now. Tell them to wait till I come back.'

His teacher shook her head. 'I can't do that,' she said. 'You must decide, and if you want to see the film you must let them take over.' Tony frowned. 'I must see the film,' he decided. 'It might be places I went to and I want to see that big mountain again.'

When he returned to the group the chalet was finished. 'That's not right,' he criticised. 'It should have a green roof and those step things are all wrong too.' His teacher intervened. 'When you went to see the film,' she said, 'you let the others take over. You left them to decide about the colour of the roof and where to put the steps.' Tony turned this over in his mind. 'All right,' he agreed at length. 'It's fair because I saw the film. Anyway it looks like one I saw in the film.' Tony had accepted the outcome of his decision and in doing so had taken a major step towards emotional maturity.

Chapter 10

Growth of creativity

There exists in each one of us the instinct to originate, to handle materials and use them in a purely personal way. Long before the young child masters verbal skills he is highly articulate in his use of malleable materials, and pioneers of modern practice, such as Marion Richardson, recognised the value of encouraging children to express their impressions in non-verbal forms. Today the child's creative instinct is at the heart of modern method, and it would be difficult to find a school in which young children are not offered experience of expression in the arts.

While the majority of teachers make good provision for the child's creative inclinations, there are many who try to decide for the child what he shall create, and place the emphasis on 'making something.' The results are put on show, and material which doesn't end up as part of the show is thought to be wasted. The idea that creative materials should be put to good use is not always the child's view of his materials, and we need to understand the growth of creativity in the young child in order to interpret his efforts realistically, as otherwise the creative process may be impaired and bring him little benefit.

We provide the child with materials such as clay and wet

68 (Yardley, A) →

sand, constructional materials such as wood, bricks and junk, marking materials such as paint, pencils, wax crayons, charcoal and felt pens, together with opportunities for bodily movement, dramatic play and experimentation with musical sounds.

The child sees in his materials opportunities to symbolise his interpretation of experience. In his earliest years he is more concerned with expanding his experience and communicating it to himself by translating his impressions into some tangible form than he is with putting experience into a form which is communicative to others.

The four-year-old who has just been on his first visit to an airport spends much time and energy trying to recapture, through the use of his own body, the shape and movement of the planes. He may also use paint to simulate shape and action, often as though he were thinking in visible form. He may be convinced that what he creates represents what he experienced, but he may have little interest in preserving the results of his efforts.

The three- and four-year-old is not much concerned with realism. The objects or materials which he selects to act as his symbols may bear no obvious relation to what is being symbolised. In his tea party, for example, grass and wooden cubes are used on any surface to represent food. But the five- and six-year-old likes to use real objects, and he prefers small versions of adult equipment for his house play. Milk or water will serve as 'tea', but it should be poured from a small tea-pot. The six- and seven-year-old becomes much more interested in detail and, given the opportunity, will make real tea to serve from his pot.

The teacher's first job is to provide as wide a range of media as possible. Creative media should be maintained in good condition and be readily available at all times. When the child first enters school at the age of four or five, he may use his materials in a highly experimental way, and from the adult point of view he may sometimes seem to misuse or even waste them. The child is now in his scribble stage of representation, and what his materials mean to him may be clear in his own mind, but by no means obvious to the onlooker. His painting, for instance, follows his thoughts and takes on the shape of ideas he has in mind. He uses the same piece of paper to show himself travelling in the car to the seaside, having a picnic on the beach, and riding on a donkey after his meal. The painted symbols may be entirely obliterated by brown 'rain,' or white 'mist,' and the teacher who snatches away his picture before it falls beneath his brush is interfering with the child's creative experience. Teachers in one nursery school no longer display children's work because they believe that the creative experience is internal to the child while he experiments with his materials, and the end product is of little account.

During the next stage, more definite form begins to appear in the child's representations. This is attributed by some adults to the child's growing knowledge and control over his materials. To some extent this is so, for if an older child, previously deprived of some material such as paint, is introduced to it for the first time, he usually passes rapidly through the exploratory scribble stages in using paint before handling it with an eye for form.

Growing knowledge of the material is, however, only part of the story. The six-year-old is entering a stage in representation when he needs more realistic symbols, and he tries to match his symbols to his sensory experience of objects. The faces he draws are given ears. Mother is given a skirt and perhaps a neck. Her hands acquire fingers and sometimes attention is paid to the number of fingers on each hand.

Many children build up a repertoire of symbols which they use over and over again. A child may design a certain personal symbol for a tree, a bird, the sun, himself, etc. Sometimes he adds to his store symbols learned from other people. Adults who teach children how to draw tend to limit the child's imagination by fixing certain symbols and as a result some children always draw, for example, a row of lollipops to represent a garden.

Daniel, aged six, became obsessed by symbols representing the human form and adults were astonished by his lewd drawings of naked women. These they attributed to Daniel's precocious interest in sex, when in fact his brother, whom he worshipped, had taught Daniel how to draw exaggerated female shapes.

The child's developing interest in symbolism is also evident in his use of waste materials, sounds, gestures, etc. A note on a chime-bar may be used in dramatic play to represent a band, or a piece of velvet may be repeatedly used to represent an important person in collage pictures. Although such symbols are not the real thing, they do to some extent echo reality.

This trend towards realism becomes more clearly defined in the creative activities of the six-year-old. The shoe-box is now given a pointed roof before it is accepted as a house. Trucks and cars made from boxes must have wheels that turn, and the observant teacher makes sure that suitable wheels are included among the odds and ends in the junk box.

The seven-year-old enters a stage when he tries to make his symbolic lorry resemble faithfully the one which he sees on the building site, and would like to drive himself. Now wheels must be fitted to an axle, and the dashboard is decorated with miniature controls. If his teacher can find him a steering wheel he is delighted. One reason for the popularity of Matchbox models is the attention paid to detail.

At this stage, the child who is working in clay, or some other plastic materials, needs help with techniques which enable him to finish his models with some precision. Little men are given eyes and even eyelashes. Model dolls who possess a complete wardrobe, have real hair, eyelashes and lifelike figures are tremendously popular with girls of seven or eight. The proud owner of one such doll spent the whole of an afternoon combing, curling and setting her doll's real hair.

In a vertically grouped class, where children at different stages in their development work and play side by side, it is interesting to note that the proximity of seven-year-old play has little influence on the creative expression of the younger child. Unless they are dominated by direction from the adult, children pass through clearly definable stages in their creative growth.

In their creative use of materials children express a sequence of ideas rather than a single premeditated idea. The younger children rarely hold in mind an image of what the outcome of their efforts shall be. Fingers and bodies become part of their flow of ideas, and the materials that they are handling get caught up in a total creative experience in which what happens to the materials is only a part of the whole creative act. The fragmentation of experience into an object to be displayed is an adult concept of creativity.

A group of children aged five to seven were taken on a visit to an airport in the Midlands. None of the children had previously visited an airport, and for some of them it was virtually their first pleasure outing by coach. A few in each age group were somewhat overwhelmed and kept close to the teacher, or one of her student assistants, throughout the visit. The majority soon lost their initial sense of awe when they entered the reception hall and were eager to investigate everthing within reach. Others chattered speculatively during the coach journey and asked innumerable questions as they were taken round the airport and out on to the balcony to watch the arrival and departure of planes. It was difficult to persuade some of these to go into the café, where the teacher had arranged for them to have orange juice and biscuits. One group of girls showed more interest in the powder room, with its adjacent nursing room, than in the spectacle from the balcony, and visiting the toilet was a popular activity. Two of these girls later transferred their attention to the air hostesses in their smart orange bowler hats, and careful note was taken of the role of one of them in organising the departing flight.

Anxious to assess the value of such visits, the teacher and students made carefully recorded observations of the children's reactions both during the visit and throughout the following days. As far as some children were concerned, the visit seemed to leave little immediate impression, and it was several days before evidence of reactions to the experience became apparent.

About fifty per cent of the group came into the classroom on the morning following the visit and immediately began to communicate their impressions in various ways. Some of the more verbally articulate children chattered volubly about the visit to anyone who would listen, while others found alternative ways of being articulate. The younger children turned first to dramatic play and bodily movement. Aeroplanes zoomed round the playground and the milk cart was loaded with luggage. Three five-year-olds assembled small chairs and spent much of the morning on their imaginary bus. One wanted to be a conductor, but the others objected because 'we didn't pay money on the bus'. Apart from this incident, the bus play was highly fantastic and much time was spent in finding willing passengers to 'sit in twos'.

Making aeroplanes was by far the most popular activity on the part of six-year-old boys. These ranged from simple designs made from two pieces of wood to elaborate models made on the junk table from cartons and other containers carefully selected according to their shape. A few models were given wheels, propellers and wing flaps.

Seven-year-old boys were even more ambitious, and two of them settled to the task of fixing tail lights with the aid of a bulb and battery set. These planes took nearly two weeks to complete and the boys asked for 'proper paint' to add detail to their models.

Two seven-year-old girls decided to make orange bowler hats

and, because they could not find anything suitable in shape, they set to work with papier mâché modelled over a plastic basin. With great care and patience they managed to reproduce the turned-up brim and added an elaborately decorated badge. 'They had an H on theirs,' the girls explained, 'so we used our own initials and then all the passengers will know our names.'

It was interesting to note that not a single child turned immediately to writing as a means of communicating his impressions. Few children, indeed, used any form of marking on paper, and it was several days before the younger children turned to painting or drawing, and a few of the older children to writing. When the writing finally developed, the quality of it reflected the value to the child of re-creating his impressions in non-verbal form before finalising them in words on paper. The boys who wrote about aircraft, for instance, were really knowledgeable about details of the planes and about flight procedures. The girls who had concentrated on making bowler hats wrote highly imaginative stories about their future careers as air hostesses.

As far as even the youngest children were concerned, attempts to express their ideas on paper were greatly enhanced by their dramatic experience. The impressions of the bus journey were vividly portrayed, and the background to the buses included glimpses of the airport and the aircraft, which obviously had not gone unnoticed. The value of non-verbal creative opportunity in the experience of young children must not be underestimated.

Through their creative activity children convey what they know rather than what they perceive. They try to communicate their own impressions and thoughts, which may bear little resemblance to what they are trying to represent. In dramatic expression the observer may be shown what the child understands about a situation, a person, or an event. In portrayals of the teacher herself, for instance, we are often surprised to see her represented as the strict ogre with a cane who sits the children in a row and lectures them, when this is not what the children have seen in school.

Such interpretation stems from what a child understands of the information that he has gathered, often before he comes to school, from an older brother who tried to scare him with awesome stories of teachers terrifying small children, or from funny cartoons or films which he has seen on television. The child may make little attempt to portray what he actually sees and hears until he reaches a more advanced stage in his ability to handle symbols.

At all times throughout the early years of life creativity is a means of deepening experience and not an attempt to put on a show. There are schools where teachers recognise this and show respect for what the child originates, not by taking it from him and pinning it to the wall, but by sharing his own view of the experience which brought his creation into existence.

Chapter 11

The growing spirit

In providing for the child's development we tend to think in terms of his body and mind. The environment is designed to satisfy his physical, intellectual, emotional and social needs. Many teachers acknowledge those other needs of the child, essential yet difficult to define, and often referred to as 'spiritual'.

The freedom of the modern classroom enables teacher and child to work together within the context of a very intimate relationship. They get to know each other very well indeed, yet the sensitive adult grows increasingly aware that there is a part of each child which always remains beyond reach or comprehension. Sometimes we may glimpse the child's growing spirit, and when this happens we are filled with humility and respect.

It would be difficult to make specific provision for spiritual growth, for how can we ever know what fosters it? Perhaps the best we can do is, by understanding what we may of its nature, to learn to establish for the child a helpful climate in which his growing spirit can flourish.

Spiritual development is concerned with awareness of self and awareness of others, the relationship between the child and others, and his growing appreciation of being alive. Knowledge of self enables the child to be aware of and understand others, and this mutual awareness prepares the ground for successful relationships with other people. The child's ever expanding knowledge of his physical world and of the people he meets in it is his means of coming to appreciate life and all that being alive involves.

Growing up is the child's major job, and the process involves him in a state of constant conflict between his developing awareness of self and of his world of inner reality, and the demands made on his attention by the external world. These two aspects of the child's world may seem at variance, and yet they are interdependent, and the individual must ultimately find some means of reconciling the two.

Eddy, for instance, is being brought up in a home where there is little privacy and where property belongs to the community. Ownership depends on the ability to appropriate and Eddy's idea of the world is of a place where possession is the reward for cunning and strength. In school he comes up against an entirely unfamiliar point of view. The book he is given to draw in may not be invaded by another child's crayons. On the other hand, he is not allowed on any pretext to take and use a book belonging to another boy, nor is he allowed to hide in his box one of the picture books kept in the reading corner. Eddy's inner idea of the world is challenged, and these new realities must be fitted into the ideas which he has already formulated; otherwise he will find it difficult to survive in the new community. Throughout his life, Eddy will meet conflict situations of ever increasing complexity and in a sense will never reach a state of complete equanimity.

The child of four or five is well aware of himself as a separate entity. What he knows of himself he has learned partly from others and partly through the way in which he is able to handle events. One child may know that he is 'a well-built boy for his age', a 'cheerful little chap', and capable of carrying his mother's heavy shopping bag. Another child may know that 'he's always ailing', 'a real little misery', and that he always gets the worst of a tussle.

The child's self-concept rapidly expands on entering school, and here he is shown his self in comparison with many other selves. One of the teacher's first jobs is to help the child to develop a realistic view of himself and to find in that self someone whom he can like and respect. Sometimes there is much a teacher must do before a child can like what he knows of himself, and gain enough confidence in himself to deal with life in a positive way.

Unless the child likes and respects himself, he is in no position to like and respect others. Children who do not like what they know of themselves react to other children in a number of different ways, each of which prohibits the development of satisfactory relationships.

Joe is the least favoured member of a family of tough little boys. During the first five years of life he was pushed to the wall, and in school he found that this was not allowed. Instead of responding with gratitude because he was given an honoured place in the group, he turned on other children the pent-up resentment of his early years. There were children here whom he could dominate, and he treated them as he was treated by his own powerful brothers. He made no friends and had a disharmonious effect on the group. It took a patient year on the part of his teacher to show Joe that he could find pleasure and satisfaction in a sensitive relationship with others.

Tina has a poor view of herself for very different reasons. She is the youngest in a family of five, and there is a six year gap between Tina and the other children. She is cuddled, nursed and petted by the rest of the family, and has come to think of herself as a helpless baby whose life is entirely organised by others.

On entering school Tina's attitude to other children brought out their protective instincts, and she was treated by them as they would treat a doll. Sometimes Tina scowled or sulked when she began to realise that she was missing some of the fun, but she made little attempt to stand on her own feet, or to resist the smothering attention of other children. It was always Tina who became the patient in hospital play. It was Tina who served as a dressmaker's dummy when Christmas hats were being fitted and decorated. It was Tina who was pushed around in the doll's pram. Her teacher had a job every bit as problematic as that of Joe's teacher, and Tina remained an antisocial, under-achiever throughout her school career.

During his first months in school the child grows increasingly aware of other people. He is intrigued by the behaviour of his teacher, or of the boy who has just arrived from Hongkong. He tries to imitate what he observes and so gain insight into what it feels like to be another person. Dramatic play is particularly helpful in developing the child's awareness of others and the teacher provides plenty of drama opportunity. The house corner and dressing-up equipment have an important contribution to make and merit the same care and attention as is paid to provision for other major aspects of the child's curriculum.

Awareness of others helps the child to understand and respond to the needs of another person, and to realise that there is a point of view other than his own. Paula and Stewart decided simultaneously to play with the construction set. An initial squabble was settled by the teacher, who told them, 'You can play with it together.' 'I'm building a house,' said Paula firmly, 'we start like this.' Paula set out some base bricks to form a square, and clearly expected Stewart to work to her idea. But Stewart had a mind of his own. 'It's not just that shape,' he said. 'It wants a garage bit at the side like this.' 'Not enough bricks,' Paula replied, 'that's too big.' The two children glowered at each other. 'Well we can take a bit off the end.' Stewart shortened the length of the house. 'Then it'll be a bit less long, but it will have a garage as well.' Paula stared at the new plan. 'It'll do,' she agreed.

The argument continued as the children constructed their house. As it took shape they began to acknowledge each other's ideas and even to consult one another before making a fresh move. The teacher listened with some amusement, but left them to work out for themselves the give and take of a human relationship.

The observant teacher encourages children to share and to work together, but she does not expect them to be consistent in these matters. Nor does she expect friendships to be stable. She may expect a child to co-operate with her sometimes, but not all the time. Throughout this stage the child's behaviour fluctuates; sometimes he is completely egocentric, while at other times he glimpses the satisfaction of considering others even before himself.

The child's ideas of human relationships develop within the context of his relationship with his physical world. Curiosity keeps him constantly enquiring, and when the teacher provides an environment which challenges and satisfies his curiosity the child's discoveries lead to further investigation. The child's concept of time is immature. He remains blissfully undisturbed by any sense of the urgency of a closely synchronised world. Time for the child is now. He has all the time in the world to stand and wonder, and curiosity and wonder colour his view of the world.

The timelessness of childhood is conducive to absorption. In a helpful environment the child readily responds and becomes entirely caught up in a human relationship, or in wonder of what he finds in his physical world. The child forgets himself, either because he is absorbed in the wonder of the first falling snow, or because giving pleasure to a friend becomes more important than seeking his own pleasure. When this happens, the child has entered a further stage in spiritual growth—that of self-forgetting.

Although the adult cannot make a child feel good, she can recognise the moment when his experience reaches towards the sublime and enable him to savour such moments to the full. Sometimes the earnest adult is so intent on encouraging the child to pursue and practise skills which will be good for him that his experience of delight, as when the first warm sunshine of spring caresses his cheek, is brushed aside as an interruption. The child then feels that the adult disapproves of his pleasure. He learns to hide his delight, or to suffer a sense of guilt if he gives way to it.

An incident which took place in Mrs Denman's classroom is typical of many. Mrs Denman hurried her own two children off to school and collected the new reading apparatus which she had stayed up half the night to finish. Her class of seven-year-old children would be juniors in seven months time, and there were still a number of them who had little idea of how to tackle unfamiliar words. Then there was the reading test administered by the headmistress just before Easter. Its purpose was two-fold: to assess the effects of Mrs Denman's teaching on the children's previous score, and to provide some guidance in grouping children during their first year in the junior school.

Mrs Denman bustled about the classroom in preparation for an early start. Practising for a week or two with these flash cards and reading games would bring Tony, Peggy and Timothy, and perhaps one or two others, up to scratch. Tony and Peggy were early. They rushed over to the windowsill where the bowls of bulbs, so carefully tended through the winter, were rapidly swelling their green cones. There was complete silence for a moment, and then Tony and Peggy ran to Mrs Denman. 'It's come,' Tony whispered. 'It wasn't there on Friday and now it's come and it's beginning to be pink.' 'I can't smell it yet,' Peggy shrieked. Both children ran back to the windowsill to see whether the hyacinths were beginning to emit their scent.

Other children entering the room were drawn by the excitement, and Mrs Denman thought it was time to intervene. 'The bulbs won't go away,' she said firmly. 'Take off your coats and then come over here. I have some games and I want to show you how to play them.'

The children dawdled in the cloakroom corner, which was situated near the windowsill. They obviously expected to see the green candle growths suddenly become pink and fragrant before their eyes. The sun now tipped the thrusting cones and the bulbs basked in a pool of warm light.

Mrs Denman worked hard trying to make the word games interesting. In a literate society children must learn to read as soon as possible; later on, when they enjoyed reading exciting books, the children would be grateful to her for showing them how it was done. Attention, however, was definitely divided, and as soon as she left the reading group, Tony and Peggy were by the windowsill in a flash sniffing the first pale pink.

Mrs Denman took two firm steps towards them and stopped. Tony caught her glance, looked guilty and sidled back to his seat. Peggy paid no attention. Her eyes were closed and Mrs Denman could tell by the expression on her face that the lovely hyacinth scent had entranced her. Mrs Denman didn't move. How could she destroy this moment of enchantment for the child? It would be sacrilege. The children had waited through the winter for such a moment. The reading apparatus would be there tomorrow, but this moment of sublime appreciation could easily be destroyed. She joined Peggy by the windowsill and bent down to enjoy the perfume herself. Tony, no longer feeling guilty, returned along with Timothy, and rapture was intensified by being shared.

Many teachers and parents have a wonderful aptitude for sensing and sharing a child's response to those things in life which make it worth living. They do not hurry the child when he wants to fondle a scrap of fur, or to lie on his back on the grass watching the April clouds chase one another across the sky. They find time to take their children to the park and to notice the reflection of winter trees on the silent pond, or to let a child glimpse the forest of moss under the magnifying glass. They provide opportunities for the child to revel in scents and sounds, exciting tactile experiences, exotic tastes, and the vista of hill and sea. They build up for the child a world of simple beauty, obtainable in even the most drab surroundings. Displays of lovely things in a school are not there merely to decorate, but to stir and reach the child's spirit and to help him to glimpse that other dimension of life.

Young children have a natural urge to make and originate. The provision of creative materials allows the child to appreciate this wonderful gift of being creative, but only when he is free to explore the uses of his materials in ways which are uniquely his own. The art materials in one school are inspirational and well maintained. The headteacher has a flair for using materials, and visitors to the school are immediately impressed by spectacular walls and alcoves. 'Isn't it lovely for the children to be able to make these beautiful butterflies,' one of the visitors said, indicating the decorative mobiles. His companion frowned. 'I wonder how so many children managed to make these wings exactly the same size and shape and then cover them with identical patterns?' he observed. His companion answered briskly. 'Because they've been well taught,' and the matter was dropped. Were those butterflies brought into being by force of the child's imagination? Did the child's natural gifts have anything to do with it?

Imagination plays an important part in spiritual development, for it is often the only available guide when we enter those realms which reach out beyond what we can fully comprehend. Every child has imagination and can be helped by the adult to cultivate the uses of it. Through adults the child gains access to works of the masters, whose imagination and inspiration caught and held people to such an extent that man has made them immortal. We may also help by leaving room for the child's imagination. We provide materials and equipment which interest, evoke curious exploration, or suggest possibilities to the child, but we avoid providing equipment which leaves him nothing to think out for himself.

The quality of the child's sensory experiences has direct bearing on the kinds of images which he forms and on the extent to which he creates with the images which he possesses. Rich visual, aural and tactile experiences leave the child with images, and they also help him to recall previously formed images and to fit them into a fresh context. This type of experience is the food of imagination, for imagination depends not on the metaphysical, but on impressions retained as a result of physical experiences.

However much we reason about children, there is always something in our relationship with them which leaves us with unanswered questions. The mind of a child works in mysterious ways. At times children seem to have access to a world which we have forgotten and which some of us barely discovered. They may not apply logical thinking as a means of interpreting events, but they have an instinct for coming near to the elusive truth. They have a natural ability to reach through to the heart of things and the greatest thinkers of our time recognise this. Those of us who work with children may share their spirituality and often grow as a result of it, if only we are humble enough to let children show us the way.

Chapter 12

Keeping and using records

The present-day emphasis on discovery methods and individual learning makes record-keeping even more important than in the days when a formal syllabus provided a step-by-step check list against which we could measure a child's progress. Teachers today work alongside their children, sometimes teaching them over two or three years, and they get to know them very well indeed. They have developed great skill in retaining and using their mental impressions of individual children, and can usually offer reasons for a child's behaviour or level of performance. But written records are also essential, and how and what we record reflects very clearly our view of the child and the way in which we plan for his learning.

A number of factors characterisitic of the present-day educational scene complicate the task of record-keeping. Schools are organised in a great variety of ways, and keeping track of an individual child in a vertically grouped or open-plan situation is often extremely difficult. Families are becoming more mobile, and frequent changes of school represents a factor of our changing society. More and more demands are made on the teacher in a time when we are fully aware of the total nature of education.

Not only is she responsible for each child's personal and academic development in school, but is also expected to teach him within the context of what happens to him outside school.

Important as record-keeping is, it should not take up an undue part of the teacher's time and energy. It must be reasonably simple, speedy and efficient. It must not dominate the learning situation, nor give rise to anxiety between the child and his teacher. In this chapter we shall examine some fundamental principles which determine the kind of record which we keep and consider in some detail the content and organisation of different types of records.

The way in which we measure the child's progress is inevitably bound up with our knowledge of the child and with the aims and objectives which determine the plans we make for his upbringing. Developmental knowledge of the child enables us to provide a well-structured environment in which his learning may progress. It also acts as a realistic guide in observing and assessing the effects of our provision. It is the child himself whom we seek to assess, rather than what he achieves or produces. How far has he progressed in his personal developmental pattern?

There was a time when local authorities designed and published standard record cards which the teacher was required to complete, and these followed the child from school to school and stayed attached to him throughout his school career. Emphasis was placed on recording standardised progress in achievements in the 3 Rs, the child's medical history and, almost as an afterthought, what was referred to as his 'personal development'. While these record cards had their uses, many teachers found them limiting and inadequate. They did not fit into what was happening in the classroom, and teachers either compiled more adequate records alongside these, or discarded them altogether.

What, for instance, did a teacher record about a child like Freddy? Freddy's home was in a very poor part of the city. On his first day at school, his mother shoved him towards the teacher. 'He's all yours,' she said. 'I've washed him, but he's always got a snotty nose. He's the weakling in the family and he takes after his uncle Bill who's a bad lot. You'll not make much of him, but I'd be glad if you'd keep him out of mischief. I've enough on my hands already with the three young uns.' The teacher smiled at Freddy, who stood in the middle of the room, a thin, weedy little chap, hanging his head. He obviously saw himself as a weakling and of no good to anyone. What he knew of himself he didn't like, and there was not much hope for him in this hostile world.

During his first day in school, Freddy refused to leave the security of his chair. He threaded beads or built bricks and, although his teacher applauded his efforts, he flatly refused to handle marking tools or creative materials. The unfamiliar space of the large hall terrified him, and when it was time for Physical Education he hid under his teacher's desk.

Then one day his teacher found something with which he felt familiar. 'Will you carry my handbag, please Freddy?' she asked. To her delight he acquiesced and trotted after her round the room, carrying her bag. 'If I go out of the room,' she said, taking him a stage further, 'I sometimes forget my handbag. Will you make sure I always have it?' She had now at least persuaded him to leave his chair and follow her to the hall.

A month had passed and what had she achieved? There was much more to be done for Freddy before he had the confidence to make marks on paper, or become interested in printed symbols. As an individual Freddy had made a major step, but by comparison with others in the class he had nothing to show.

The kind of records kept by a teacher must provide for children like Freddy, as well as for the normal and sometimes gifted child at the other end of the scale.

In Britain teachers have unique freedom to design their own curriculum, modes of organisation, and the general life-style of their work in school. They have the opportunity to develop their own beliefs about the job, and their enthusiastic efforts have generated enlightened ideas in which many other countries are interested. Education has become a very intimate and personal business between teacher and child, and how each teacher records her work is likewise her own decision.

Before designing her modes of recording, the teacher must be clear about her basic philosophy. Does she really believe that her work centres on the idea of helping the child to develop his unique abilities as naturally as possible, to formulate his own beliefs and attitudes, and then have the opportunity to live by those beliefs? Or does she fundamentally see herself as a tool of society through whose administrations the child acquires social skills? In the first case, records of the child will focus mainly on personal and social development, and in the second case on academic achievement.

While the details of the recording must be left to the teacher, there is a general framework of observation within which most teachers can operate.

At least three types of record are needed in a progressive first school: the record maintained by the headmistress which refers to the development of the school and its philosophy in general; the record kept by the class teacher relating both generally to her class group of children and specifically to individual children; and the record kept by each child of his own progress and achievements.

Each of these is equally important. The headmistress is ultimately responsible for the type and suitability of the educational opportunities offered to children in her school. She may extend considerable freedom to each teacher and by so doing make her own job of co-ordinating the work of her team that much more difficult. She alone is able to assess the value to the school community of individual enterprise and contribution. She blends the various ingredients into a harmonious pattern.

If she is to keep educational development alive in her school, she must initiate as well as support, and it is only through keeping track of the ideas and materials which she feeds into the enterprise that she is able to assess, to encourage or discard, and generally to formulate a guiding philosophy which forms the stable core of the community.

This core philosophy is not static. It is the result of constant discussion with all members of the community. It is frequently revised and modified to meet the ever changing needs of the school. In the well-maintained records of headteachers we can trace the evolutionary growth of revised procedures, and modern practice owes much to such records kept during the last fifty years.

The class teacher needs to observe each child as an individual, but also as one of the group. Her on-going diary of what happens to the group of children whose names appear on her register will include all major interests and events, and general developmental trends such as her relations with parents, the introduction of a new method, or a drive towards improving the mathematical content of the environment, etc. A forward and a backward look are essential aspects of this diary. It should also include comments on the introduction of new materials, with notes as to what happens to them. It constitutes, in short, tangible evidence of the way in which she structures the life of the group as a means of enabling individual development to take place.

The teacher's record of individual children should contain her own summary of the child as a person on entering her class, his attitudes to learning, social and emotional adjustment and intellectual possibilities. This summary will combine her own estimation along with evidence from previous records of the child. Her on-going observation of him will be designed around her assumption of what he should acquire in the way of competence and skills, and this will be based on her developmental knowledge of his personal and cognitive growth. Many teachers find a desk jotter, on which they note anything significant as it occurs, an invaluable aid. The teacher usually tries to record exactly what the child said or did, rather than talk about him. These notes can later be transferred to her personal record book, but are likely to be forgotten if not recorded on the spot. It is often at the end of a week or so that the significance of a recorded incident becomes apparent.

From his first days in school, the child can keep a permanent record of his own achievements and development. This may take the form of a folder containing examples of his work. It could be a personal jotter in which, with help from his teacher, the child records his discoveries. Both will enable visiting parents to watch his progress. The individual diary is also something which can be taken home, and a record such as this is invaluable in helping parents to understand the full significance of the child's activities. 'I blew up a balloon. I balanced it before I blew it up and after against some grains of sand. I had to add more sand when it was full of air. Air has weight.' This is much more communicative than the verbal explanation, 'I played with a balloon'.

In some schools, class record charts of reading and number attainment are filled in by the children, but teachers who believe that the child should concentrate on improving his own skill rather than competing with his peers find no purpose in such charts, nor in awarding stars, points and the like.

Even in the freedom of the modern classroom progress can be recorded step by step as well as in global terms, and comments such as 'Ian is an intelligent boy who adjusts readily to his environment and enjoys the more challenging situation . . .' need to be qualified by precise observation.

A teacher could, for instance, enter in her record the comments, 'David showed an interest in money . . . David's concept of money is improving . . . etc.' Or her record could read like this:
    4.11. 'My new coat cost a lot of pennies.'

5.2. 'Me and Billy's playing shop and we want silver money and penny money.'

5.9 'Why is paper money more than this nice silver one?'

6.0. 'My Daddy buys money over the counter at the bank.'

6.4. 'I had some money at Christmas. I bought a battery for my signal set and I had money left, so I put some of it in my money box and I've still got a bit for chocolate.'

6.7. David set up a bank. He made coloured paying-in slips, cheque books and notes of different denominations. 'I don't need pennies and things,' he explained. 'I'm only going to deal in big money.'

In the days when teachers worked to a syllabus, the check list which it provided could be used as a measure of the child's achievements. While the free-range learning of present-day schools has made nonsense of a syllabus, teachers still need to have a clear idea of what to expect of children at each stage in the educational system. The teacher in the child's first school may give priority to his growth as a person, but his intellectual development remains her ultimate responsibility. If he is to adjust to modern society he needs to be conversant with literacy and numeracy skills, and what the child achieves in these is still a major concern of most teachers. The difference between today and yesteryear lies in the way in which a teacher constructs her measurement scale. Today she thinks in terms of appropriate steps leading to realistic goals for individual children and does not expect each child to measure up to some hypothetical norm.

Preparation for teaching involves the student in a rigorous study of child development, and the knowledge thus gained becomes a teacher's main guide in devising suitable steps and measurement tools for each aspect of the child's work. Where reading and writing are concerned, experienced teachers are usually extremely perceptive with regard to the various skills and sub-skills, and seem able to hold in their heads a general progress chart by means of which they are able to check each child.

Where the development of mathematical ideas is concerned, they are not so certain. The pattern of mathematical concepts is complex, and many teachers need help both in devising suitable check-up situations and in interpreting observations.

In Chapter 7 we analysed a number of mathematical ideas and outlined the pattern of their growth in the young child's experience. Such a pattern may serve as a guide to the teacher in dealing with other aspects of cognitive development. We could take the idea of length, for example, and draw up a step-by-step outline of its progress. Words relating to ideas of length are acquired by the child in his early speech, and he relates these words in a limited way to personal experience. Evidence of his understanding is reflected in his spontaneous use of words such as long, shorter, tallest, etc. The next step is to compare one length with another, and then to put various lengths in order. The use of the child's own body as a means of comparison soon follows, and some children have reached this stage on entering school. During the next stage the child perceives the value of using unmarked sticks and tapes as a means of deciding 'how much?', e.g. the length of a strip for a headband. A child may be six or seven before he realises the significance of using standardised units, and he will need much experience of these before he understands the reason for having large units and smaller ones, and the relationship between the two. By the time he is seven, the child should be able to estimate with some degree of accuracy the length of both straight and curved lines. The use of scale may be outside the range of ideas available to the child during his first school years.

This step-by-step developmental pattern enables the teacher first of all to devise situations in which the child will meet an appropriate idea, and then to suggest a means of assessing the stage which he has reached in understanding. By pinpointing his degree of understanding in any particular idea she will know what he has already assimilated and where he must go from there, and will have some idea as to the stage which he should have reached in his understanding of other mathematical ideas. For example, a child who is capable of estimating the length of a piece of string to within a few centimetres should be able to estimate roughly the weight of an object which he can hold in his hand. Differences in competence may be the result of experience, and this suggests a gap which the teacher can fill.

Developmental knowledge is equally helpful when assessing the child's social and emotional growth. Experienced teachers are usually very skilful in using their knowledge for this purpose. They quickly decide whether a child is 'emotionally mature', or 'not well-adjusted for his age', whether his behaviour is 'acceptable', or indicates 'some degree of instability'. When they do this they are applying a scale of behavioural terms in much the same way as the application of mathematical terms described above.

This use of developmental knowledge is of far greater use to the teacher than assessment by published tests. Test material which helps the teacher to identify and diagnose a child's problems in reading, for example, has an important part to play, but tests which simply provide a score are time-consuming and even misguiding unless thoroughly understood. Developmental scales, on the other hand, are flexible and show where the child is rather than what he has achieved. They are therefore particularly helpful to the teacher who works in a school where vertical grouping and open-plan teaching situations emphasise the individuality of children and necessitate very personal ways of assessing them. It is the child's personal development which is measured rather than his score on a normative scale.

When recording in this way, dating entries, or noting the age of the child, are important, for this enables the teacher to assess the rate of growth as well as the stage reached. The following extracts from Simon's record illustrate the way in which his teacher observed his developing concept of time and so found help in planning for progression within his classroom experiences.

4.10. At 10 a.m. I told the children to put on their coats as we were going across to the school hall for service. I caught Simon making off through the school gate. 'I thought it was time to go home,' he said, 'when I put on my coat.'

5.1. Simon drew a picture of himself eating his breakfast, running to school and having milk . . . all in the same picture.

5.3. 'Why do you always say "Just a minute, please" when you're busy? What's a minute?'

5.6. 'It's going to be Christmas. Not the next week, but that other week after.'

5.8. 'It's time. The bell's just gone.'

T: 'When did it go?'
'Oh! One minute ago.'

5.10. 'Both hands are pointing straight up. It's time to go.'

5.11. 'Please can I help David to paint the box so's he'll be a bit less longer?'

6. 'I'm six today and do you know I had a birthday last year and I'll have a birthday every year when June comes.'

'My birthday is on June the sixth and I'm six years old . . . do I count the day I was born?'

6.1. 'My Dad went fishing. He started at eight and he finished at seven.'

T: 'That was a long time wasn't it?'
  'Yes. About twelve hours.'
T: 'A whole of twelve hours?'
  'Well not quite. About eleven hours I should think.'
6.1.   'It stays light when I go to bed. Why is it light a long time in the summer?'

Studying this record we are left in no doubt about the relationship between the developing ideas of a child and the structure which this requires in the learning situation, in whatever type of school the child may be.

The use made of records is every bit as important as maintaining them. In the first place, the actual job of recording involves the teacher in close observation of the individual child and leads to greater understanding of him and his problems. The actual task of writing comments down helps the teacher to clarify her interpretation of what she observes. It also helps her to retain what she notices and so to build up a sound concept of the child himself. It is reassuring to the teacher to find that even amidst the free-flowing of learning in the modern classroom she is able to watch over and keep track of the individual child, and teachers are often surprised, when it comes to making entries, about the amount and quality of their contact with the individual. Teachers have become so skilful in catering for the needs of children that they might remain unaware of much that they do if their conscious attention were not drawn to it.

In a vertically grouped class, the teacher obviously maintains a continuous record throughout the span of a child's life in the school. If she works in a team-teaching, open-plan situation, other members of staff will contribute to her record, but in the first school children normally remain attached to one member of the team, and it is she who will write up the comments of others in the team. The concept thus gained of the child will be a more composite one.

When a child moves from one school to another, or from class to class in a school, the question arises as to the value of passing on the record. In the freely organised school, teachers usually know most of the children in the school community and prefer to build on their personal contact and assessment of the child when he enters their class. Even when the child is not known, some teachers prefer to start from scratch and to get to know the child through their own impressions rather than those of others. Some teachers find it helpful to build up their own relationship with the child first, and then refer to previous records.

When a child transfers from one school to another he is making a dramatic change in his background and school situation, and reactions relating to one set of circumstances may be irrelevant in another. This is true to some extent of any change made by the child, and a summary rather than the full personal record of another teacher may be sufficient. Any decision made should be in the interest of the child, as a means of ensuring for him a fair deal in a fluid learning situation.

Chapter 13

Parents are part of the plan

Peter is six. He is a well-built, energetic boy who throws himself wholeheartedly into anything which catches his interest. At the moment he is completely absorbed in finding all the ways in which he can make a certain sum from the coins in front of him. As he reaches a solution he draws round the coins, and when his paper is full he takes it to his teacher. 'I never thought it'd be all that,' he tells her. 'Can I do another one of those next time?' His teacher smiles. Peter loves school and he is a most rewarding pupil. 'That's very good, Peter,' she says. 'Of course you can.' Peter glows and for the moment his sense of satisfaction and the approval of his teacher matter more to him than anything else in the world.

Ten minutes later Peter is making his way home for tea. When he reaches the building site he pauses. The bricklayer is having his tea break, and Peter takes up an imaginary brick and a trowel and lays the next row of bricks along the wall. He mutters to himself as he works, and the words he uses are certainly not those which he hears in school.

At about half-past four Peter bursts into the kitchen where his mother is changing the baby. Peter looks over her shoulder.

'She's getting big,' he says. 'She's as long as the towel. Will she get as big as me?' Assured that she will, he pursues the enquiry. 'I eat dinner to make me big, and tea. She just has drinks out of a bottle. How can she get big?' His mother's explanation is interrupted by the demands of her youngest child, so Peter eyes the table. 'I'm hungry,' he announces. His mother shakes her head. 'You'll have to wait till I've given Betty her milk,' she says. 'Go and play with the others for a bit.'

Peter joins his two older brothers in the tool shed. Mike, the elder brother, complains. 'You can't come in. We're doing something and it's not for kids.' Peter has learned how to solve this kind of problem. Some secret thing is happening in the shed and he must be included. 'Mum said,' he threatened. 'I'll go and tell her if you don't let me in.' The ruse works. He is sworn in and allowed a single pull on the grubby stub of a cigarette.

Tea-time brings these experiments to a halt, and after tea the boys follow the televised adventures of their hero in an exciting Western. For the rest of the evening their dramatic interests converge, and the most bloodthirsty parts of the story happen all over again.

The day finishes in helping Dad to fill in his pools coupon, each son in turn selecting names from a bowl. It's Thursday and Peter knows that they all think about money on Thursday, because one day they'll be rich and he will have a large sum for pocket money. There are so many people in Peter's home and not much money to go round, and this makes it a most meaningful commodity, which is one of the reasons why he enjoys the money games in school. At 7.30 p.m. Peter settles in the top bunk and dreams of the day when he will spend all his money in the big store because Dad has won the pools.

What Peter learns in school is but a very small part of his total learning. Nevertheless, that small part is essential, in the way that a pinch of salt or a measure of yeast can be essential, and if what happens to him in school fits into the pattern of his life outside school, then planned education becomes doubly effective. Peter has been learning from birth. During his first four years, learning was more rapid than during any other comparable period in his life. When we face facts we realise that Peter, like each of his companions, accomplishes up to ninety per cent of his learning outside school. He learns from every person he meets and in every place in which he settles, but always, for good or ill, what he learns in the home and from his family has a most powerful effect on him.

If we are to obtain for the child learning conditions in which his abilities are maximised, we must respect the contribution made by the parents. Moreover, we must see the role of the parents in perspective. It is arrogant to assume that the school's function is to compensate for the ineffectiveness of some parents and that we are authorised to tell parents how they may be allowed to help. Few parents are failures. The majority do what they can, and many do an excellent job. In every case it is of the greatest use to the child to establish a partnership between home and school in which parents and teachers play *reciprocal* roles.

While the majority of parents are anxious to co-operate, many are very uncertain of how to set about it. Teachers have ample evidence of the importance to the child of parental attitudes. Some teachers spend a great deal of time and effort telling parents this, but do they always want parents to co-operate on equal terms? Are teachers sometimes jealous of their skill? Do they sometimes endow their work with a certain mystique, in which secrets are revealed only to the skilled practitioner? Do they sometimes suggest that parents may help only up to a point, beyond which the secret techniques of the trained practitioner must take over?

The teaching of reading is a case in point. There are still a great many teachers who warn parents that help with reading will damage the child's chances of learning reading skills. Parents are an essential part of the educational structure and they should not be made to feel that what they do will interfere with the teacher's work. Teachers have gone a long way towards improving the home and school link, but there is still much to be done about helping parents to co-operate if the fullest benefit to the child is to result from that link.

To begin with, parents need to be fully aware of the rapidity of learning in the early years. Few of them realise, for example, that fifty per cent of the child's total intelligence has developed by the time he is four. They know how rapidly he grows out of his clothes, but are not always aware that his social development is equally rapid, and that the relationships that he forms in the home act as a basis for learning to live among others and work with them for the rest of his life. They know that he has a will of his own, but may not realise that what he will be as a mature person is determined to a considerable extent before he enters school.

In the same way, parents know that they teach the child to speak and are proud of him when he does so well, but few really understand the significant part played by speech at every stage and in each aspect of the child's learning. Some parents are aware that the child is learning 'something' when he 'helps' in the kitchen or in the garden, but few of them realise the importance of the foundational ideas established during these play experiences.

Parents with widely differing home circumstances were asked what they thought their children learned at home. One harassed mother replied, 'I keep her clean and she gets plenty to eat and I see she's in bed by eight o'clock, but with six to look after there's no time to teach 'em. Anyway we send 'em to school for that.'

'I expect my children to learn about books and arithmetic in school,' one knowledgeable mother explained. 'I think it's up to parents to teach children culture. I take mine to art galleries. Lynn spends Saturday morning at a ballet school and John is learning to play the piano. These are the things children should learn to enjoy, but it's up to the teacher to get them through exams and into a good job.'

'I always let Alan help when I'm doing things,' a very thoughtful mother admitted. 'You see, he really enjoys making cakes and washing up so long as I don't hurry him. He talks about what he does and seems to remember what I tell him. I suppose that's a sort of learning, and he'll be a father one day so he might as well learn about things in the home.'

One father, who was a joiner by trade, had his own workshop alongside the garage. 'Young Brian's my partner already,' he said. 'I let him use some of the tools and show him how I get the sections to fit together. He'll learn something about mathematics from me because he only learns about numbers in school and it's problems he finds interesting.'

Several parents felt it their duty to teach children 'good manners' and 'how to behave towards one another and towards other people', so that 'they get on well when they get to school'. They also felt it important to 'teach children good habits such as cleaning their teeth and keeping clean'. Some were more concerned about teaching their children 'to stand on their own feet', or 'to stick up for themselves', because 'they won't always have their parents and they must fend for themselves if they want to get on in the world'.

The words of a mother who lived in a poor part of the city expressed what many tried to say. 'I've brought up four,' she said simply, 'and I think the most important thing they learn has got a lot to do with the home. They're all different and I want them to be themselves. We've done what we can, me and Bill, to help each of ours to be a person.'

Parents can learn a great deal from one another and there is sometimes much teachers can learn from them. Discussion with parents offers by no means a one-way benefit, and yet it is obvious from these replies that many parents underestimate their contribution to the child's development, and some seem to think that intellectual development takes place only in school. Time spent on helping parents to understand the part which they play is a good investment, for everything which we do with the child when he enters school must be grafted on to what he brings with him. It must also relate to what he continues to learn in the home during his school years.

The child's ideas about books and reading, for instance, may be soundly established by the home, and what the home does about the printed word makes all the difference to the child's progress in both his initial reading and in maintaining the development of his reading skills.

Parents may read to their children, but they often need help if they are to do it well. Observing the way a teacher handles a story book may give a parent some useful clues. Some parents do not understand the importance of sharing books with children, or do not feel that they have any part in the reading process. 'They learn to read when they go to school,' said one parent. 'I can't see any sense in giving them more of it at home.'

On the other hand, there are many parents who are only too willing to help their children with deciphering skills, yet are afraid to express their interest because they have the impression that what they do will interfere with the teacher's approach. Some teachers positively foster this notion and much benefit is lost to the child when what is called for is guidance rather than prohibition.

What is important is that the parent should help in the right way and with the right frame of mind. Sharing with children their own pleasure of books, reading to them, involving them in reading recipes, instructions, television programmes, letters, notices, and generally encouraging them to take part in all the essential literary activities of daily life are essential functions of parents.

Child and parent together can make friends with words, looking at the beginnings and ends of them and at similarities in their patterns. Words are exciting and interesting symbols, and knowing them as such helps to establish good attitudes towards print. Children can learn how to handle books long before they enter school, and even before they are able to interpret the symbols they can be shown how the message is obtained from the print. Parents can introduce children to poetry and good literature. These and many other reading interests should be part of the loving relationship which exists between parents and child.

On the other hand, parents need to know that anxiety, drilling the child as a punishment for failure, and senseless practice at reading from books like the ones from which the child learns in school are detrimental to reading progress. With guidance from the teacher, however, parents can help the child to develop many basic reading and number concepts and skills, which can be transferred to the materials and methods which he meets in school. Moreover, parents and teachers together establish the emotional context within which reading takes place, and the mental activity of reading grows out of these emotional conditions.

Another area in which parents need help is in answering children's questions, and often in talking to them, or talking in their presence. Some parents think it a waste of time to answer a child's questions and feel that what is said in his presence 'doesn't matter at this stage', as the child 'hasn't learned to think yet', or 'doesn't take much in'. What they may not realise is that although the child does think, he hasn't the words or skill in handling sentences to enable him to express his thoughts.

Parents can contribute a great deal to the development of the child's thinking and communication skills. The central importance of language to intelligent human thought and learning has been expounded recently in extensive research (see *The Psychology of Language, Thought and Instruction* by John P. De Cecco. Holt, Rinehart and Winston, 1967). Parents need to understand their essential role in early verbal play and verbal interaction. The child's language skills develop as a result of reaching towards the skills of his verbal superiors. Talking to other children is not enough, and in the early years of life it is the parents who provide verbal stimulation.

Parents who talk to their child from the moment of birth and who respond to his vocal sounds and reinforce, with the use of facial expression and gesture, his efforts to communicate, are helping him to shape his speech sounds and promote basic communication ideas. Some parents believe, as one mother expressed it, that 'it's no good talking to her until she can understand. She'll learn to speak in her good time and if she's like the others, once she starts she'll never stop.' What the mother failed to realise is that talking nineteen to the dozen is not a symptom of adequate thought.

Not only should parents talk to their child, they should talk to him about what is happening. When he is in the bath, for instance, the child notices the behaviour of the water, the soap, steam, his towel, etc., and mother's simple commentary, in which he should be encouraged to join, helps him to formulate ideas about splashing, wet and dry, floating and sinking, soft, smooth, slippery and so on. Similarly, and at a more advanced level, he may share verbally as well as visually his father's efforts to repair a sewing machine, make a kitchen table, or diagnose a fault in the engine of his car. Vocalising in association with parental attention forms an excellent basis for later speech usages.

Another important way in which we can help parents is in developing constructive attitudes to their children and to what they learn. There is no harm in parents being ambitious for their children, providing this does not lead to anxiety and the establishment of unrealistic goals. Many parents, endowed with a natural knowledge of psychology, are well aware that tension and anxiety on their part have an adverse effect on their child. They may try to veil their anxiety and wonder why this does not help very much, for suppressed emotion is readily communicated between parent and child. If they can be shown how to develop positive, helpful attitudes, expressed in such ways as making reading experience an exciting and pleasurable event, or comforting the child when he feels a failure, and altogether generating a beneficial emotional climate in which the child feels able to make the best of himself, then their child will feel supported by those two pillars between which he grows.

Many children suffer in school because they are emotionally too bound up in their parents and home. We all know the mother who finds it hard to let her 'little one' go, who smothers him with affection, or who dotes on him until the emotional burden is too much for him to bear. Home and parents should act as a stable rock from which the child feels safe to adventure. Merely telling a mother not to cling to her child, or to try to make him emotionally independent, is not enough. She needs to be shown how to do this, and even the most clinging mother can be helped to understand the sense in teaching her child to fasten his own buttons, to be left in the care of another adult, or to forget himself and his problems by becoming interested in things to do.

In some schools these problems and others are dealt with in a series of discussions with parents before the child enters school. In one school mothers are encouraged to help for an hour each week on a rota basis, and they then join a discussion with teachers about events of the week and how they have been handled. In another school parents are offered a workshop course in which they are acquainted with the materials used in the teaching of reading and mathematics, and with the methods employed in teaching basic skills.

Many schools try to involve parents by asking them to help with parties and outings, to mend and make equipment, to provide waste materials, or perhaps to talk to the children about their jobs. Most schools hold consultative sessions, or open days for parents. Useful as these arrangements are, parental participation should amount to much more. Parents have an essential part to play in the child's intellectual, as well as social and emotional development. Teachers and parents should be able to work together on equal terms. Education for parenthood is perhaps a future hope. Meanwhile, society leaves it to the school to take the lead. This is highly important work and a responsibility allowance or a special appointment might help the work along.

Chapter 14

Developing the uses of language

This chapter on language comes at the end of the book not because it is less important than any other aspect of the child's growth and development, but because language is seen as central to the learning pattern and so much a part of the fabric of the child's life as to seem inseparable from all that he is doing. Because the teacher needs to be aware of the ways in which it develops all the time, a final reminder seems appropriate.

There are many existing theories of language, and much concern and controversy arise as a result of malformed notions which stem from ill-digested theory. Bernstein's ideas, for example, have been grossly misrepresented and many people have claimed that he has 'proved' the language of working-class children distinctly inferior and therefore a handicap in school, when he has certainly said no such thing. *The Language of Primary School Children* by Connie and Harold Rosen (Penguin Education for the Schools Council, 1973) is a report which came out of a project initiated by the English Committee of the Schools Council for the Curriculum and Examinations in England and Wales. Teachers who wish to deepen their understanding of language development will find excellent guidance in this report.

A group of five- and six-year-old, so-called linguistically deprived children were chatting vigorously to one another in a corner of the school cloakroom. They were hushed and hurried into the classroom where a 'remedial' teacher was preparing to enrich their language experience with the aid of plastic fruit and a pre-planned programme of responses. It would be difficult to imagine an experience more removed from the real lives of these children. While there may be some value in helping children to elaborate their uses of language through formal programmes, it must certainly not be at the expense of the language which they already possess, and if a child is subjected to a programme which makes no attempt to use the speech with which he is familiar, it is doomed to failure or at best to short-lived improvement of a very superficial kind. Teachers in socially impoverished areas are well aware that, although the child is not ultimately bound by his home language, he must start with it, and any tuition offered to him must take into account both the way he speaks and what he does with speech.

As in all that which the child learns, language development is a process of continuity and expansion. It starts with what the child already possesses in the way of speech and vocabulary. We have seen throughout this study how the child uses the language he has for his own purposes, when he is given the opportunity to learn in ways which come naturally to him. The problems arise when the adult tries to make the child use language for purposes that are not his own. He may need to learn how to shape sentences according to the rules of grammar, to use words in socially regulated phrases, or to write a formal essay or letter. But this comes after he has explored the use of words in his own life.

In the early stages the child gives little thought to the way in which his own language is to be viewed by others. He talks as part of his dramatic expression of his own impression of people and events, or uses words as a link between himself and what he is doing, as part of his thinking, or as a means of giving shape to his feelings. When he begins to understand words as things which can be represented by visible symbols as well as aural sounds, he treats them in much the same way, and in his first attempts to write the child is unaware of the many rules which govern the structure of the written word. If he is harassed at this stage by an adult who sees the rules as more important than the reasons for writing, the child may very well lose interest and even avoid what he sees as a chore required of him for the benefit of others. Later he will understand that the rules are there to help him in his purpose, and much depends on the sensitivity of the teacher in knowing when to offer tuition.

Throughout this book, in many examples of what goes on between teacher and child, we have seen how the teacher ensures and improves language development by participating in what the child is doing. Much is done intuitively, yet most teachers would agree that the quality of the help given improves when it is consciously thought out. Some important questions then arise.

In the modern classroom much of the child's learning focuses on the dialogue between him and his teacher, and the problem of how to lead the child on in thought has no single, simple solution. When to ask a question, when to comment, when to withold either of these, and when to answer the child's questions and which is the best way of doing so are decisions which the teacher makes constantly throughout the day. There are really no rules, and the way the teacher responds is the result of awareness and understanding on her part, of the role language is playing in the particular situation in which she is involved. The following incident may serve to illustrate this point.

Simon, aged six, drew a picture in which the sun, moon and two round objects were clearly discernible. Beneath his picture he wrote, 'My two stones'. Knowing Simon, his teacher sensed that he was puzzling out some problem and she asked him,

'Tell me about your two stones.'

'Well, you see, the sun and the moon go up and down in the sky and they have to have a stone to pull them.'

'They have a stone each?'

'Yes. That's the stone for the sun and that's for the moon'.

Simon was satisfied with his fantastic explanation and his teacher simply commented. 'Have you seen the stones?'

A few days later, Simon brought his picture to show her again. 'It doesn't need the stones,' he said. 'When the sun goes down it pulls the moon up.'

'We'll watch what the sun does every day when it shines,' his teacher suggested. Careful observation of the path traced by the sun and the moon followed and Simon's original notion that there was a connection between the two was greatly expanded.

Such skilful use of dialogue develops partly as a result of experience, but also because the teacher understands the nature of the child's thinking and the stages through which he develops ideas of cause and effect. In situations such as this knowledge becomes understanding and is available as an invaluable aid in developing classroom practice.

In conclusion

The work being done by teachers in Britain has stirred interest in many parts of the world. Many of our schools are excellent examples of the way in which education has been opened up to meet the extremely individual needs of young children, and teachers in these schools have every right to feel proud of what has been achieved.

While the context within which learning takes place has been established and the foundations of a sound educational system have been truly laid, there is much to be done in structuring the total edifice before the work of recent years can be brought to fruition.

Teachers know that every part of the structure must be carefully designed and equally carefully thought through. The size of their task will seem overwhelming unless they are given time to do their thinking and some basic guidelines to work to.

At the time of writing the promise of improved in-service facilities for teachers seems likely to be fulfilled. Teachers are to be given time within their contract to study the job which they are doing and to work out their ideas. The co-ordination of teachers' efforts calls for leadership of a very high quality and through their own impressions rather than those of others. Some the Professional Tutors will play a key role in planning and administering for the studies of their colleagues.

Teachers themselves must take the initiative in determining the qualifications, status and function of the Professional Tutor. The vast experience of practising teachers must be used as the basis for future developments, and teachers must not hang back, allowing non-teaching specialists to plan their practice for them.

We have seen in this book how much the practising teacher already knows about the structure of the child's learning. The next step is for them to analyse what they now do intuitively and to make use of their own experience to strengthen and deepen the situations which they provide. If structure is not attended to, the free-flowing life of the modern classroom will be under attack and brought into disrepute by those who are only too willing to identify and expose its weaknesses.

At the moment the results of improved practice are erratic and sometimes blurred. Here and there they are proven, when what we need is evidence so widespread and confirmed that it cannot be denied. Modern practice has yet to prove itself as universally sound and the teacher, who is at the core of it all, is the only person who can bring this about.

Help from other sources

The education of young children is the concern of many types of people. Teamwork between trained and experienced teachers, inexperienced teachers, playgroup leaders, nursery nurses, parents and social workers provides the context within which the child's learning takes place. The following recently published works have been selected with their very varied needs in mind.

Fundamentals in the First School by M. Brearley and others. (Basil Blackwell, 1970.)
We have grown to expect of the Froebel Institute a lucid exposition of sound ideas and this is a good example of Froebel Institute teamwork under the leadership of Miss Brearley. It sets out to help teachers and teachers in training to understand what they are doing and to interpret knowledge of children in their own way. It is 'mainly concerned with the process of learning and the principles on which we base our teaching'. These same principles are defined and applied to many areas of experience, ranging from science and mathematics to music and morality.

Each chapter follows a similar pattern. The developmental

process in each aspect of learning is related to the provision made for the individual child, and emphasis is placed on the responsibility of the teacher for intervening in the child's learning, when appropriate, in order to foster development.

The writers urge teachers to 'try to isolate and examine their own professional ideas' and to teach according to their own beliefs. Motivation is regarded as fundamental to effective learning. Great attention is paid to the 'personal uniqueness' of children, the continuity of their learning, the importance of co-operative effort and shared experience, and the significance of the way in which each child shapes his own mind as a result of interaction between the world of external things and his own inner experiences. Many examples of good practice illustrate the way in which these principles may be applied.

This study presupposes a sound knowledge of child development and of present-day practice on the part of the reader. Good photographs and illustrations illuminate the text, and a useful glossary and a selected bibliography are included. It should prove a source of inspiration and guidance to all who aim to make their teaching more effective.

Discovery Learning in the Primary School by John Foster. (Routledge & Kegan Paul, 1972.)

John Foster writes from his personal experience as headmaster of an infant and junior school. 'The fundamental purpose of the primary school,' he says, 'should be to help children to think for themselves, to exercise choice, to make judgements, and to discriminate.' Music, movement and manipulation he regards as fundamental in motivating children towards the use of the three Rs. His aim is to analyse and evaluate the contribution of discovery learning through describing the work of children as individuals, in small groups, in classes and in the school community as a whole. The role of the teacher is depicted as one of positive involvement in both planning and developing discovery work.

John Foster pays particular attention to the problems of organisation, emphasising the need for structure and progression. 'It is essential', he writes, 'that good records should be kept because it is through accurate recording that the picture of a child's progress is built up.'

The ideal teaching style, he points out, will vary from person to person. 'I do not believe there is any one system of organisation which will ensure success', and 'an understanding of the principles' is of far greater use than a model.

He includes a list of suitable children's books, suggestions for background reading and for discussion points for teachers. For the inexperienced teacher or the teacher who would like to change from a formal approach, this book offers specific and constructive guidance, while the experienced teacher will appreciate its rigorous appraisal of present-day discovery methods.

Learning in the Primary School by Kenneth R. Haslam.
(George Allen and Unwin, 1971.)
Probationary and student teachers understand modern theory, but have little experience of how to apply it in the reality of a busy classroom. They need advice on many matters which may seem trivial to the experienced teacher.

Kenneth Haslam believes that 'it is in the small details that we lay the foundation of the learning situation'. As the head of an infant and junior school with twenty years' teaching experience, he is well qualified to understand the problems of inexperienced teachers and to offer them valuable advice.

This book is packed with sound advice and every point is illustrated through the actual work of children. Mr Haslam covers the approach to every aspect of the curriculum, including classroom and group organisation, behavioural problems, record-keeping, relations with parents, the use of tape and film, sources of books and equipment, and suggestions for further reading.

While not all would favour Mr Haslam's somewhat inconsistent approval of concerts, nativity plays for parents, end of term reports and loads of assignment cards, its realism will be warmly appreciated, particularly by the beginner.

Alongside the Child in the Primary School by Leonard Marsh.
(A & C Black, 1970, and Harper & Row, 1970.)
This book outlines the professional responsibilities of teachers working with young children, challenging them 'to take a second look at some of the educational theories which they use to guide their work in the primary school'.

Quality of feeling is more important than intellectualising for the young child, and Leonard Marsh is deeply aware of the significance of the creative process in learning. It was in the field of art, he reminds us, that 'the children's personal experience was first considered as the focus for the curriculum of the primary school'.

Talk and paint are the means by which a child may deepen experience. Literature stirs the emotions and the imagination. The creative process is a great deal more than evidence of self-expression. Personal discovery which is 'aimed at ensuring that children have a wide and varied experience out of which will come understanding of ideas' is not the same as merely 'learning about' something.

Learning through imitation, Leonard Marsh believes, involves so much of the emotional life of the child that its fundamental contribution becomes apparent to the observer, and what absorbs the child educates him.

He interprets learning as the child's means of coming to terms with his private world, and the teacher's role is 'to come alongside the child, his language and his experience.'

This perceptive survey of the contemporary scene will 'provide discussion material for teachers and students' and it constitutes a serious attempt to bridge the gap between theory and practice.

Being a Teacher by Leonard Marsh.
(A & C Black, 1973.)
In this book Leonard Marsh takes up the basic theme of his earlier book, and the role of the teacher participating in the experience of the child is closely examined. 'Teachers make the schools what they are, and the quality of our education depends on their competence.' His main intentions are to make the teacher think deeply about his role and to indicate the growth of theory from practice.

'The essence of education,' he says 'is the practical activity that takes place in the classroom,' and we must be clear about the true meaning of what it is to be a teacher. We need to get behind the labels such as 'integrated day', 'team teaching' and 'child-centred', and examine the precise function of the teacher as he participates in the child's learning. 'The teacher is the most vital element in the environment of the classroom.'

Leonard Marsh illustrates his points by describing in words and photographs a two-hour sequence with one teacher, and so provides a pattern of teacher behaviour with which the reader may identify. He also pays attention to the contribution of non-professionals in the community school.

In developing his thesis, Leonard Marsh assumes a depth knowledge of the teacher's job on the part of the reader, and experienced teachers will find this study particularly helpful.

Understanding the Young Child and his Curriculum by Belen Collantes Mills.
(Collier-Macmillan, 1972.)
This comprehensive overview of the young child and his curriculum contains a selection of papers by leading authorities in a number of fields. The theme of this symposium focuses on a thorough re-examination of the purposes of education in our democratic society. Schools exist to meet the needs of society's children and the curriculum should be designed around what they are. The curriculum serves too often as an instrument for traditional miseducation, and its content is determined by what children *can* learn rather than by what is essential. The emphasis is on speed, and on urging the child towards some adult goal.

This book is written with the American teacher in mind, but there is much in it which relates to the work of British teachers. It falls into three sections, and each chapter is prefaced by questions.

In section one, contributors provide insight into the characteristics of young children. Anna Freud, for example, points out that children hold a point of view which is often at variance with that of the adult. Lovell stresses the need for the child to take an active part in experience, and he reminds us that Piaget has shown us that merely submitting to experience does not enable the child to restructure his thinking. Another contributor emphasises the importance of pre-school stimulation in the intellectual development of the child. Play is fully acknowledged as the quintessence of the child's nature and as essential to cognitive growth.

Section two provides guidelines for the foundation of a more effective curriculum and contains an excellent study of language learning. In the third section, various systems at home and abroad are examined and evaluated.

Playing, Learning and Living by Vera Roberts.
(A & C Black, 1971.)
The fruits of thirty years' experience enable Vera Roberts to offer sound advice on every aspect of nursery school education to the many types of people who work with the pre-school child.

Playgroup leaders, nursery nurses in training and probationary infant teachers will find this book a mine of information about matters affecting young children, from mathematical thinking and spiritual experience to wet pants, swearing and biting.

Vera Roberts lives very close to children. She stresses the importance of human relationships and the need to respect the child and treat his efforts with understanding. She reinforces her advice on behavioural problems and in keeping control of the group by referring to her own experiences with children.

Experienced teachers may feel that much of this advice, e.g. that tools should not be used as weapons and sand should not be thrown about, is plain common sense, yet someone needs to advise the uninitiated, and advice on such simple matters is often neglected to the detriment of the child. While the book deals in depth with language work, not enough attention is paid to the child's thinking experiences and cognitive development.

Even so, this book offers important guidance to beginners.

A Child's Eye View: Piaget for young parents and teachers by Mary Sime.
(Thames and Hudson, 1973.)

Piaget and his findings are well known to teachers, but how far they are understood and profitably used is another matter. Books about Piaget are difficult to read and many young parents, playgroup leaders and others involved with the upbringing of young children have neither the vocabulary nor the thinking habits of the trained educator. They are perfectly capable of grasping Piaget's theories when they are explained in simple terms, but it is difficult to find an educational writer who can communicate difficult ideas clearly.

Mary Sime sets out to bring the results of Piaget's research to those most in need of it. She succeeds in introducing the spirit of Piaget through describing the work of her students and colleagues with young children. She selects a few key points made by Piaget and brings them to life with the help of descriptive text, photographs, diagrams and reproductions of children's work. She succeeds in making Piaget's work intelligible to anyone who can read, and by so doing justifies yet another book on Piaget.

Her study brought Mary Sime to some important conclusions. 'It leads me to realise,' she writes, 'that, in every matter, every day, every child will have a point of view different from my own.'

The child's point of view is the only one from which his thinking can grow. It should not be disregarded.

Although her observations are restricted to children of students and college staff, and deal mainly with mathematical and scientfic thinking, this book is highly readable and provides a unique study of the child's intellectual growth.

Index

Other titles in the Evans Modern Teaching series

Resources in Schools by R. P. A. Edwards describes the nature and use of the school resource centre: how it can be designed, administered and staffed, its library, audio-visual and retrieval functions, and its central role in the life and work of the school. Numerous illustrations show apparatus and existing resource centres in operation.

School in the Town by Barbara Blit looks at environmental studies as a developing part of the primary and middle school curriculum. It is written particularly for teachers of children in the 8 to 13 age range, and offers a practical programme full of useful ideas for the study of their environment by children in urban and suburban areas.

Parent-teacher Partnership by Graham Bond poses fundamental questions regarding the desirability of parent-teacher co-operation. The author, who is a recognised authority in the field, discusses beliefs and attitudes, considers the many problems met by teachers and parents, and offers ideas and solutions which vary according to the different backgrounds of the people concerned.

History with Juniors by Michael Pollard outlines a modern approach towards teaching history to junior and middle school children. Various projects are discussed, always in practical terms, including the use of archive material, local history sources and field work, and the author describes the relationship between such projects and other curriculum ideas.

Sums for Today by Gordon Pemberton presents a cogent argument in favour of the new methods of teaching elementary mathematics, using concrete, structured materials. The author establishes that traditional methods, stemming from practices of Victorian ledger-clerks, are irrelevant to today's situation, and give the learner little understanding of the concepts of calculation. He also establishes, using many illustrated examples, that the new methods are mathematically based, essentially practical and easy to understand.

Learning about Life by Mary Lane demonstrates the significant role sex education can play in the primary and middle school curriculum. The author shows that a child-centred approach contributes to

117

all-round development and a child's sense of identity. She suggests teaching methods for different age-groups, gives guidance on answering children's questions and problems of parental co-operation, presentation of facts, etc., and concludes with a survey of current literature and audio-visual materials available for teachers, children and parents.

When Children Learn by David R. Boorer attempts to answer some of the basic questions on the psychology of teaching. Central issues such as creativity, motivation, intelligence, personality and the learning process itself are discussed, and where there are conflicting theories, points 'for' and 'against' are summed up briefly. The practical problems of the teacher or student teacher are considered throughout the book, which keeps technical jargon or terminology to a minimum.

Also by Alice Yardley

Young Children Learning

This series is designed to express, as clearly as possible, current educational theory in terms of the practical work of teachers and children in infant schools. The four books in the series incorporate the most recent research into the ways in which children develop and learn. They are illuminated throughout by plenty of factual examples from classroom situations, and each book covers a range of topics connected with some particular aspect of the child's life in school. Not only teachers, but parents and students in colleges of education will find these books a constant source of inspiration and guidance.

The individual titles are *Reaching Out*
Exploration and Language
Discovering the Physical World
Senses and Sensitivity

The Teacher of Young Children

The demands made upon the teacher of young children are many, varied and increasing, and to be effective she needs to evaluate them, to plan her working and to establish her own order of priorities. This book helps the reader by examining the work of practising teachers and by suggesting practical solutions to some of the teaching problems.

Young Children Thinking

The aim of this book is to provide simple practical suggestions for adding intellectual dimensions to the curriculum. It is not through the addition of subjects and exercises that this can be achieved; it is more a matter of examining the quality of what already exists, of exploiting the events of the day and finding in them a means of stimulating greater mental activity. In this book Alice Yardley clearly demonstrates how to realise this very desirable aim.

Learning to Adjust

The nature of children's behaviour, in all aspects, is of great importance to every teacher since, whether it be 'good' or 'bad', it affects the basic relationship on which education depends. In this book, Alice Yardley considers situations which are likely to challenge the teacher of young children by illustrating them with examples based entirely on the work of teachers over the past twenty years. The reader obtains, therefore, a realistic picture of the many difficulties, problems and opportunities which face experienced and less experienced teachers alike when dealing with young children, a picture which will help her in her own teaching situation.

The Infant School

An outstanding study which illustrates the latest beliefs and practices in early childhood education by focusing on first-hand observations of developments in infant schools of different kinds over the last fifty years. All the information given in this book was obtained from teachers practising during this period. A glossary of popular educational terms is included, and the author illustrates the way in which, as revised ideas have emerged, new descriptive terms have been employed to identify practices associated with them.